SLAVISTIC PRINTINGS AND REPRINTINGS

edited by

C. H. VAN SCHOONEVELD

Indiana University

299

THE PETRAŠEVSKIJ CIRCLE

1845-1849

by

JOHN L. EVANS

Florida Technological University

1974

MOUTON

THE HAGUE · PARIS

LIBRARY OF CONGRESS CATALOG CARD NUMBER: 73–81081

Printed in The Netherlands by Mouton & Co., The Hague

ACKNOWLEDGMENTS

I am deeply appreciative for advice given to me by Professor Clifford Foust at the University of North Carolina, Chapel Hill. Also I would like to thank Professor Joseph Anderle of the University of North Carolina for making key suggestions about my writing style. Professor Sergei Zenkovskii of Vanderbilt University gave valuable encouragement. My students at Stetson and Florida Technological University gave much moral support to allow me to carry out the project. Finally, my wife Banning helped me with the original proofreading.

J.L.E.

CONTENTS

INTRODUCTION

Russia in the 1840s would never have qualified as a fertile bed for the germination of the seeds of socialism. The public character of the country formed a classic example of the 'closed society' as adumbrated by Karl Popper.[1] By edict of the Minister of Education, Sergej Semenovič Uvarov, intellectuals were subjected to the official ideology of orthodoxy, autocracy and nationality. Prior censorship requirements made extremely difficult the open expression of novel or divergent notions. The imposition of the authoritarian ideal upon the individual was enforced by the army and the bureaucracy. The debasement of the finer human qualities, which Popper suggests is common to such closed societies, manifested itself in the ruination of many of the outstanding Russian intellects of the period.

Yet many of those intellectuals who withstood the intimidations of the forties were becoming conscious of themselves as men set apart, as part of a yet unidentified intelligentsia. They were drawn and held together, not only by their gentry backgrounds, but also by a common sense of alienation from their government. The *Petraševcy*, colleagues and followers of Mixail Vasil'evič Butaševič-Petraševskij, were one important group of such men.

The first signs of a general intellectual awakening in the ranks of the gentry had been seen in the latter eighteenth-century protests of Nikolaj Novikov and Aleksandr Radiščev. They were the first to criticize openly the evils of tsardom – Novikov through journalism, publishing, public education, and philosophy, and Radiščev primarily through *A Journey from St. Petersburg to Moscow* (1790), the famous commentary on the iniquities of serfdom for which Catherine banished him to Siberia. But these two and their followers – Ivan Petrovič Pnin among them – were too few to make an effective protest before 1800; in no way did they

[1]   Karl R. Popper, *The Open Society and Its Enemies*, 2 volumes (New York, 1963), *passim*.

constitute an intelligentsia such as was defined in the latter nineteenth century. Even the Decembrists who attempted a *coup d'état* in 1825 did not represent an intelligentsia. These were largely army officers, and their revolt was an affair among gentlemen; ideas, while important to them, by no means dominated their lives.

The radical intelligentsia came into being during the reign of Nicholas I. The new generation of young gentry had come to feel alienated from the regime and from society, in part because the Tsar relied for his support not upon them but upon older, more corrupt bureaucrats. It would seem that Nicholas feared another Decembrist plot might develop were the young and volatile given freer reign. After 1825, the youth wanted nothing to do with the army, although army service had formerly been the noblest of young ambitions. The ready-made outlet which presented itself to them was the university.

In 1803, Alexander I had enlarged the network of civilian educational establishments. New universities in Petersburg, Kharkov and Kazan were added to the previously existing ones in Moscow, Vilno (Polish-speaking) and Dorpat (German-speaking). Each included a complex of secondary schools. Many such schools were also built in provincial capitals. At the same time, diocesan seminaries were reformed and modernized. Nicholas had inherited an educational system that he could not abolish.

Although established in 1803, Alexander's educational improvements did not come to fruition for perhaps, twenty, years.The number of university students remained tiny compared with the total population of the country; in 1840 there were only three thousand university students among forty million people. From these three thousand, however, came the first stirrings of protest during Nicholas's reign. Most of the *Petraševcy* were of this group.

The expression of student protest was formulated in the establishment of literary circles (*kružki*) which met to discuss common interests. These circles had their antecedents in Russia, although earlier groups were not made up of university students. In the early 1830s, Moscow University had played an important role in the formation of certain of the clandestine groups, outstanding of which was the circle of Nikolaj Stankevič, a graduate of the university. Mixail Bakunin, Vissarion Belinskij, Konstantin Aksakov, the novelist Ivan Turgenev, historians Timofej Granovskij and Sergej Stroev, and the future publisher Mixail Katkov were at one time or another members of this circle. The Stankevič circle was not inclined to revolutionary activity; it was a casually organized body that met on Fridays in Stankevič's quarters to discuss philosophy, listen to music, and read romantic poetry.[2] Edward J. Brown describes the group as "a belated and peripheral reaction to the European romantic movement".[3] Aside from their romantic inclinations, the group's chief significance was that the members discussed Hegel for the first time in Russia.

In the late 1830s and early 1840s, the influence of the German romantics waned considerably in Russia. There were two reasons for this. First, the more impressionable student youth of Russia were greatly attracted to the more practical problems of the peasantry. Beginning in the early 1840s, the peasant struggle against the regime heightened, and in 1847-1848 it reached the highest peak of the decade. The students acquired enthusiasm for the social sciences: such faculties as economics, geography, history and political science seemed to the students to give a rational explanation of the development of human society.[4] Second, the power of the ideas of the German romantics was too abstract. Some kind of positivist ideology was necessary if Russia was ever to solve its social problems. The students needed a philosophy that showed the way for all people, not for just a few dreamers.

In the early 1830s, a circle organized by Aleksandr Gercen [Herzen] and Nikolaj Ogarev appeared among the student body of Moscow University. In contrast to the purely literary and philosophical Stankevič circle, the ten members of Herzen's circle entertained political questions. Herzen and Ogarev, recognized as two of the first transformers in nineteenth-century Russia, were young men of gentry background united in their search for some form of protest against what they saw as the appalling conditions of their time. They were convinced of the need for political as well as social revolution in Russia. The German philosophers held no answers for them, and as they cast their eyes in new directions in the search for an ideology to express their protest, they were attracted by France. France had had a 'successful' revolution in 1789 and another in 1830 which was not so successful. There had been a revolt of the Lyons silk workers in 1831. Now in 1832 France seemed on the verge of a third great upheaval.

What caught Herzen's eye was the appearance in 1832 in Paris of the Saint-Simonians, whom he saw at that time as the leading revolutionary

[2] Edward J. Brown, *Stankevich and His Moscow Circle, 1830-1840* (Stanford, 1966), p. 8.
[3] Brown, *op. cit.*, p. 13.
[4] A. N. Pypin, *Moi zametki* (Moscow, 1910), p. 64.

element in the country. He read avidly of the trial of the sect in 1832. The fact that the Saint-Simonians were socialists was at first not as important to him as the fact that they had led the protest against social injustice. Herzen's "first allegiance was not to any particular doctrine but to whatever was new and radical in France".[5] But his fascination with the novelty of the French protest was soon replaced by an acceptance of socialism as an important ideology for the Russian revolutionary movement.

The socialism of Saint-Simon, Fourier, Leroux and Owen in western Europe did not represent the protest of a single class; it was much more pervasive in its appeal. In general, the different socialist schools railed against the archaic society which placed unnecessary restraints on the small capitalist.[6] They could count among their immediate ideological ancestors, Rousseau, and other eighteenth-century philosophers. The phalanstery of Fourier and the New Christianity of Saint-Simon could be traced back through Robespierre's Republic of Virtue all the way to the idealized state of Plato. The socialist systems of the nineteenth century endorsed the proposition made by their predecessors that society could be just and rational.

Both Herzen and Ogarev were drawn to socialism because each of the schools contained a moral system or code. To Herzen, socialism was much more than just an economic doctrine; it was a new way of life with an elaborate set of rules.

The socialist intellectual was protesting against the whole world. He hoped for a new world based on a new social system. In contrast to liberalism, socialism could not be contained, but must be spread over the entire world. Inherent in each of the schools was the idea of progress, with harmony as the end result. Nothing could be worse than the present, Herzen believed, so the idea of progress appealed very strongly to him. He was convinced man could not continue in the state which Petr Čaadaev had described in 1829: "We live in a narrow present, without a past as without a future, in the midst of a dead calm."[7]

Herzen was not interested in the aspect of socialism that proclaimed the abolition of private property. In fact, in the 1830s neither he nor Ogarev had developed any ideas whatsoever about the nature of revolu-

[5] Martin Malia, *Alexander Herzen and the Birth of Russian Socialism, 1812-1855* (Cambridge, Mass., 1961), p. 102.
[6] Malia, *op. cit.*, p. 116.
[7] Marc Raeff (ed.), *Russian Intellectual History: An Anthology* (New York, 1966), p. 163.

tion. But they were concerned with the development of the concept of revolution in men's minds. Unlike the Decembrists, they believed that the masses must be educated to the new world of socialism.

Herzen and Ogarev were not the only members of the intelligentsia who found an ideal in the France of the revolution. Mixail Evgrafovič Saltykov-Ščedrin wrote that "from France flowed over us the belief in humanity, from this land there shone on us the conviction that the 'Golden Age' was not behind but before us. In a word, all good, all that was desirable came from there."[8] In another passage, Saltykov brilliantly depicted the flavor of the forties in his own country:

In Russia – actually not so much in Russia as specifically in Petersburg – we existed only factually, or as was said of that time, we had a "form of life". But spiritually we lived in France. In Russia, all seemed finished; in France all, as it were, was just beginning. And not only now at this moment but the revolution had begun over fifty years ago and now was beginning anew and did not show the slightest desire to stop.[9]

Enthusiasm for the French socialists was strongest in St. Petersburg. As Saltykov pointed out, it was not the France of Louis-Philippe and Guizot that caught the fancy of the Petersburg intellectuals; they read Etienne Cabet, Louis Blanc and especially George Sand.[10] Proudhon's essay "What Is Property?" appeared everywhere in St. Petersburg. But by the early 1840s by far the most popular French writer in the Russian capital was Fourier.

With the demise of his circle in 1834, Herzen turned temporarily to Hegel, but he soon returned to French socialist thought as the solution to Russia's problems. He quickly identified Fourier's phalanstery with the Russian *mir*. He was captivated by Fourierism's basis in an acceptance of human nature as Fourier saw it, in contrast to Saint-Simon's tenet that the basic nature of man must be changed. On the other hand, he had no desire to live in a phalanstery; it was too reminiscent of Count Arakčeev's military colonies, established under Alexander I. From time to time, Herzen's inclination vacillated between Fourierism and Saint-Simonism.

But the ideas of Fourier were the ones that emerged as the ideological framework of the political thought of the *Petraševcy*. The young Russian radicals gleaned their understanding of the Frenchman's social system not only from Herzen, but also from Professor Viktor Porošin at the

---

8 M. E. Saltykov, *Za rubežom* (Moscow, 1950), p. 148.
9 Saltykov, *op. cit.*, p. 149.
10 Saltykov, *op. cit.*, p. 148.

University of St. Petersburg, whose classes many of them, including Petraševskij himself, attended in the late thirties and early forties. It is the use to which the *Petraševcy* put this understanding with which this book is concerned.

The study of nineteenth-century Russian history too often neglects the *Petraševcy*, as history generally too often fails to take due notice of courageous but unsuccessful rebels. The very fact that this little band of reformers undertook to remedy the frightful conditions in the Russia of their day demands our notice. Their efforts to change Russia from a repressive, socially and politically unjust state into an 'open society' were sincere but ineffective. They failed because the task was much greater than they had ever imagined. But an examination of their struggle lends new insight into the growth of a radical social consciousness in mid-nineteenth-century Russia, a consciousness which would in following decades demand the changes that altered not only the history of Russia, but the history of the entire world.

I

PETRAŠEVSKIJ

The Petraševskij Circle, or *Petraševcy,* constituted the most coherent and articulate opposition to the Russian Tsarist regime between the Decembrists of the 1820s and the more effective reformers of the 1860s. Nevertheless, the circle was a loosely-knit group of people bound primarily by their visits to Mixail Petraševskij's Friday evening discussion meetings and by their belief that some sort of social reform was necesary in mid-nineteenth century Russia. The *Petraševcy* represented diverse personalities and widely varying degrees of radicalism. Some were outspoken revolutionaries. Others were cautious but concerned legalists.

The man whose passionate idealism drew them all together, Mixail Vasil'evič Petraševskij, was born in St. Petersburg on March 1, 1821, in moderately well-to-do surroundings. His father, Vasilij Mixajlovič, had been schooled at the Ecclesiastical Seminary in Poltava and the Imperial Surgeons Academy in St. Petersburg.[1] His work in anatomy earned him a gold watch from Alexander I and appointment as General Bagration's chief surgeon in the Second Western Army in 1812. Attaining the rank of full doctor in 1821, the elder Petraševskij enjoyed a sterling medical reputation under Alexander I and Nicholas I. He was noted for two inventions: a machine for stretching out dislocated joints and a pressure clasp for securing opened labial arteries.

Vasilij Mixajlovič Petraševskij was in good standing with the regime. At the birth of his son, Mixail, he asked Tsar Alexander I to be godfather. Because Alexander was unable to attend the christening, however, M. A. Miloradovič, the military governor of St. Petersburg, took his place.[2] Miloradovič later died in Dr. Petraševskij's arms on Senate Square, shot by a Decembrist insurgent.

Very little biographical information is available on Mixail Vasil'evič's

---

[1] *Russkij biografičeskij slovar',* XIII (St. Petersburg, 1902), p. 633.
[2] V. I. Semevskij, *Sobranie sočinenij: M. V. Butaševič-Petraševskij i Petraševcy,* ed. V. V. Vodovozov, II (Moscow, 1922), p. 24.

mother. Her maiden name was Feodora Dmitrievna Fal'evaja. Her
father was mayor of Moscow in 1805. She comes to light primarily as
a strict, often petty mother to her five children. The only son of the
family, Mixail was constantly derided and rebuked by her. She so
vehemently criticized his boyhood habit of spending his every cent on
books that as an adult he never allowed himself more than the bare
necessities of life – which necessities, of course, included great numbers
of books.[3] Feodora Petraševskaja forbade her son's presence whenever
she had guests in the house. When Dr. Petraševskij died in 1845, leaving
his family a gentry heritage but a small inheritance, his widow ad-
ministered the estate tenaciously, demanding from her son receipts for
even the smallest sums he spent. Petraševskij later reported to the Commission that found him guilty of subversion that his mother falsely denounced him at his father's funeral: "Admire this man for a worthy
son", she said loudly. "He is glad at his father's death."[4] Maternal
rebuke and rejection followed Petraševskij all his life; his mother out-
lived him by two months.

In 1832, Petraševskij entered the Lyceum at Carskoe Selo, where
several future *Petraševcy* were educated. The school's Director, General
Gol'tgoer, maintained extremely harsh discipline and even permitted
corporal punishment which the state Minister of Education had banned.
Gol'tgoer encouraged the students to eavesdrop on one another and on
their teachers. He was generally despised by the students and few talented teachers stayed long in his employ.

In the lower grades of the school, Russia's most widely known Lyceum, the reading of foreign books was forbidden; even the older students had difficulty checking such books out of the library. The monthly
journal *Biblioteka dlja čteinja* [Library for Reading], edited by O. I.
Senkovskij, was available for reading in only one room of the library.
For most of the students this magazine – containing articles on Russian
and foreign literature, science, art, economics, and agriculture – was
the only source of literary light from outside Russia.

Young Petraševskij's relationship with his classmates was recalled
succinctly by his fellow student A. N. Jaxontov: "Petraševskij was not
likeable, he did not respond to the friendly remarks of his classmates;
he made unexpected, eccentric jokes at which none of us laughed."[5]

[3] A. V. Semevskaja, "Zametka o M. V. Butaševič-Petraševskom", *Russkaja starina*,
12 (December 1901), p. 493.
[4] V. A. Desnitskij (ed.), *Delo Petraševcev*, I (Moscow, 1937), p. 122.
[5] A. N. Jaxontov, "Vospominanija carskosel'skogo liceista", *Russkaja starina*, 10
(October 1888), p. 99.

M. E. Saltykov, later a *Petraševec* and a social novelist, reported that Petraševskij was disliked by the students and that he spent most of his free time visiting in the lower classes.[6] Konstantin Stepanovič Veselovskij recalled that Petraševskij stood out because of his strangeness. "He made the impression of an unbalanced mama's boy who was spoiled and was accustomed to have granted his wildest fantasy."[7] According to Veselovskij, Petraševskij could not bear to think of himself as average; he was determined not to be like the others.

Petraševskij appears to have been equally unpopular with his teachers. Not only did they consider his thoughts too liberal, but they also found him extremely obstreperous. One of his favorite pastimes was baiting one of his tutors, Aleksej Ivanovič Kox, a very nervous, easily perturbed man. Petraševskij amused himself by starting a conversation with Kox and then confusing the discussion with sophisms until Kox was on the verge of apoplexy.

Upon his graduation from the Lyceum in 1839, Petraševskij ranked at the bottom of his class.[8] In spite of that, or perhaps because of it, Petraševskij completely surprised Director Gol'tgoer by making a speech at the graduation exercises in which he quite soberly thanked the administration for its solicitude toward the students and at the same time urged his classmates to forget their former quarrels. The deliberate irony of the speech went unnoticed by the Director, who publicly apologized to Petraševskij for not appreciating his gifts until that moment.[9]

All graduates of the Lyceum were guaranteed admission to the University of St. Petersburg, so in 1840 Petraševskij enrolled there. The evidence of his Lyceum experience notwithstanding, he was an extremely able student, and by April 1841 he had obtained his degree from the Juridical Faculty of the University.

His term at the University of St. Petersburg was a critical time in Petraševskij's life. He was undecided about a career and he was unsure of himself as an individual. He took courses in Roman and international law and in diplomatic relations. However, it was in Professor Viktor Porošin's courses in political economy that Petraševskij found his greatest stimulation.

Porošin was a recognized figure in his field, often compared favorably

[6] Semevskij, *Petraševskij i Petraševcy*, p. 27.
[7] K. S. Veselovskij, "Vospominanija o nekotoryx licejskix tovariščax", *Russkaja starina*, 5 (May 1900), p. 449.
[8] A. Herzen, "Petrashevsky", *Revue politique et littéraire (Revue Bleue)*, XLVI (November-December 1908), p. 388.
[9] *Ibid.*

with Professor Timofej Nikolaevič Granovskij of Moscow University. Porošin openly denounced the injustices of serfdom, calling it slavery. The worst enemy of an egalitarian society was unlimited private property, he told his students, so the amount of property in private hands should be drastically limited.[10] In his later lectures, Porošin discussed the philosophies of Fourier and Saint-Simon of France, saying that only through such ideas as theirs could a new society be built. The Porošin lectures on the western European reformers were an eye-opening experience for the young Petraševskij, as well as for future Petraševcy who were also students of Porošin.

Petraševskij's revolutionary activity began at the University. To younger people asking him for books he most often recommended Father Augustin de Barruel's Mémoires pour servir à l'histoire du Jacobinisme, published in 1797-98. The Jesuit de Barruel saw the French Revolution as a result of a pre-conceived plot by Voltaire, Rousseau, Robespierre, and others. Petraševskij concluded that the lessons of de Barruel's study established the possibility of revolution in Russia; the difficulty lay in finding the means to raise such a revolution.[11] For the moment, Petraševskij opted for radical revolt, although he was later to declare himself against it.

In March of 1840 Petraševskij took a position at the Ministry of Foreign Affairs, where he remained until his arrest nine years later. He served as translator in cases in which foreigners residing in St. Petersburg had difficulties with the police. He was delighted whenever he could help free such people from the police, since he was convinced that in many instances police activity was unjust. This work apparently confirmed Petraševskij's active hatred of all injustice, a passion that motivated him thereafter more than any other drive. He was especially outraged by injustices committed against his fellow employees and at least two examples of his reaction against such injustices are worth noting.

In May 1847, Petraševskij denounced to his superior one Colonel Ivan Sinel'nikov for irregularities committed during a judicial investigation in which Petraševskij had served as translator. Petraševskij felt the defendant, Johann Luri, had been unjustly accused of embezzling government funds. The colonel had used threatening language to Petraševskij, whom he outranked, and seemed to be less interested in Luri's

[10]   V. I. Semevskij, "A. V. Xanykov", Golos minuvšago, 2 (February 1916), pp. 47-48.
[11]   Herzen, op. cit., p. 388.

guilt or innocence than in the preservation of his own prestige. Despite Petraševskij's protest, no action was taken against Sinel'nikov, nor was Luri allowed any redress. Although it gained him a reputation as one concerned about bureaucratic injustice, Petraševskij's independent attitude did little to endear him to his superiors in the Ministry.

In October of 1848 Petraševskij registered a complaint with the Department of the Senate against Police Officer Petr Zanutscy. Petraševskij had witnessed the rough treatment of Officer Aleksej Kondrat'ev at Zanutscy's hands and had instantly offered Kondrat'ev his services as a lawyer. But again 'injustice' prevailed when Kondrat'ev dropped the complaint and the Senate dropped the proceedings. Zanutscy accused Petraševskij of not being in his right mind and of being "eccentric".[12]

His determined pursuit of the unjust was Petraševskij's main eccentric trait. As a member of the government bureaucracy, he was expected to dress conservatively. Yet he walked the streets of St. Petersburg in a wide coat and a wide-brimmed hat, a veritable sombrero, which scandalized his fellow clerks. At times he sported a four-cornered hat of recent French vintage, delighting in the sensation he created. A colleague related that Petraševskij once wore a woman's dress to the Kazan Cathedral, where he stood among the women and pretended to pray. His extremely masculine physique and black beard, however, soon attracted the attention of the ward inspector, who approached him and said, "Kind sir, you are, it would seem to be, a man in woman's clothes." Petraševskij reportedly replied, "My dear, you are a woman dressed up in man's clothes." The ward inspector was so stunned by such an answer that Petraševskij was able to disappear in the crowd.[13]

The drive for originality and apartness which marked him at the Lyceum followed Petraševskij into government service. Lower level public officials were forbidden to wear beards, moustaches or long hair. Petraševskij pointedly ignored the regulation and wore his hair in curls to his shoulders. There were hints dropped at the office that he should have his hair cut. Then he was ordered to have it shorn. The next day Petraševskij appeared with long hair. As the Director prepared to reprimand him, Petraševskij yanked off a wig and revealed his completely shaved head!

Alexander Herzen's account of the *Petraševcy* compared Petraševskij to Armand Barbes, the Parisian *gamin* who went to his death at the

[12] A. V. Bezrodnyj, "K biografii Petraševskogo", *Istoričeskij vestnik*, 1 (January 1901), p. 229.

[13] P. E. Ščegolev (ed.), *Petraševcy*, I (Moscow, 1926), p. 47.

barricades in 1848 utterly unconcerned about his fate. Herzen explained that Petraševskij's eccentricities in dress and action manifested his total obliviousness to the present. Petraševskij believed, wrote Herzen, that only the future was important, for it held hope for a new Russia.[14]

By 1840, Petraševskij had come to believe that education would be the most powerful weapon in his battle against injustice in Russia. His dissertation at the university had been titled "A Theory of Education for the Youth of Russia", but he had not settled upon the best medium for the propagation of his ideas.[15] He considered founding a magazine, even going so far as to plan a lead article on the meaning of social criticism and the means for making it effective. He planned an article tracing the history of religious skepticism since the beginning of time, stating that more important than religion for the well-being of man were history, literature, political economy, and philosophy. The basic purpose of Petraševskij's magazine was to have been the awakening of the masses.[16] He solicited articles from his friends at the Lyceum, including M. E. Saltykov. He even discussed his planned venture in an 1840 article, "My Aphorisms". The magazine, unfortunately, never appeared.[17]

In the summer of 1844, Petraševskij attempted a pedagogic career. He saw teaching as an opportunity to spread his ideas among young people as he lectured on jurisprudence. He first approached Prince Peter von Oldenburg, Headmaster of the Lyceum, who referred him to the school's new Director, General Dmitrij Bogdanovič Bronevskij. Although Bronevskij could offer him no position at that time, he liked Petraševskij. But in the fall of that year, the school administration learned that two of the younger students, Aleksej Mixailovič Unkovskij and Vladimir Konstantinov, were visiting Petraševskij in his quarters. Unkovskij, who was later active in the freeing of the serfs, was then fifteen years old and had written a libretto entitled *Poxod v Xivu (7)* [*March to Xiva*] which poked fun at people in power. A copy of the manuscript was discovered in the possession of another Lyceum student. Unkovskij confessed that he was the author and was expelled. The younger Konstantinov was allowed to remain. Petraševskij's chances for employment at the school were dashed.

The Unkovskij incident upset General von Oldenburg so much that he denounced Petraševskij to the Governor General of St. Petersburg,

[14]   Herzen, *op. cit.*, p. 388.
[15]   Desnitskij, *op. cit.*, III, p. 392.
[16]   Desnitskij, *op. cit.*, I, p. 548.
[17]   Desnitskij, *op. cit.*, I, pp. 546-549.

Alexandr Kavelin. Together they concluded that it was dangerous to allow Petraševskij to remain in the city. Von Oldenburg spoke with Aleksej Fedorovič Orlov, Chief of the Third Section, and Petraševskij was put under surveillance. The agent assigned to the case reported, however, that there was only one topic of conversation at Petraševskij's house: new laws must be made for the country. Orlov, convinced that while Petraševskij was a chatterbox he was not dangerous, called off the surveillance.[18]

Thus Petraševskij's pedagogical career ended with his coming for the first time under the scrutiny of the government. Although there were surely other institutions at which his reputation would not have prohibited his employment, it appears Petraševskij chose not to pursue the teaching profession after his rejection by the Lyceum. It seems clear he was more interested in propagandizing than in tutoring students in the academic verities. He could easily communicate with the young men of St. Petersburg, whose life in the capital made them forward-looking and cosmopolitan in their attitudes. Petraševskij would probably have been loathe to relocate to another city; his roots were sunk deep in St. Petersburg, and no provincial city could offer such a gay round of intellectual circles and *avant garde* excitement.

Although Petraševskij did not write voluminously, he left one work of scholarship and several articles which are worth noting. Three of the articles were written in the late 1840s and contain his ideas on Fourierism. The work of scholarship was actually a subterfuge for getting into print socialistic ideas which could not be published openly in Russia.

In April 1845, an artillery captain named Nikolaj Sergeevič Kirilov published a work titled *The Pocket Dictionary of Foreign Words Which Have Entered the Russian Language* and carrying the cover notation: "This dictionary is a short encyclopedia of the arts and sciences, or to say more truly, a short encyclopedia of the knowledge which has been brought to us through European education."[19] Kirilov had dedicated the work to the Grand Duke, Mixail Pavlovič, brother of Tsar Nicholas and head of the School of Cadets. The first volume, including words through the letter "M", was written by Kirilov's two assistants, Valerian Majkov and Roman Romanovič Štrandman. Because they were dissatisfied with their arrangement with Kirilov, they refused to edit the second volume. Petraševskij, a friend of Kirilov, offered to assume the task.

---

[18] Semevskij, *Petraševskij i Petraševcy*, pp. 56-57.
[19] *Karmannyj slovar' inostrannyx slov, vošedšix v sostav russkogo jazyka*, 2 volumes (St. Petersburg, 1845-1846).

His appointment as chief editor of Kirilov's dictionary proved to be a stroke of great fortune for Petraševskij. The book served as the perfect vehicle for the propagation of his ideas. It bore an innocent, scholarly title and it treated words from western Europe, the cradle of the socialistic systems that most excited Petraševskij. He made use of the dictionary's established didactic tone and chose definitive phrases which helped him state the social, political and philosophical beliefs which constituted his world-view. He avoided the censor's criticism by using an Aesopic language, a vital convenience in 1846, when Petraševskij had developed a political posture quite unacceptable to the regime.

The second volume of the *Dictionary*, including the letters "M" and "O", contained 353 entries on 238 pages. Although Petraševskij is credited with only forty-three items that can be fitted onto eighty-two pages, his words carry a potent message.

A total of 2,000 copies of the *Dictionary* was printed, but the government seized 1,599 before they were put on sale. The other 401 were widely scattered. Twenty-seven were sold in St. Petersburg bookstalls, 148 were distributed to booksellers in other Russian cities and 170 were sold by prior subscription throughout Russia. Seventeen copies were seized in St. Petersburg bookstores by the editors. Thirty-two were given away by Petraševskij and the Censorial Committee kept seven copies.[20] Kirilov protested the government seizure and promised Mixail N. Musin-Puškin, head of St. Petersburg Censorial Committee, that he would delete all of Petraševskij's articles. Kirilov's petition was accepted and a censor was put in charge of the reediting. However, the task was too great. Petraševskij's articles remained in and the book remained banned. Seven years later, the Minister of Education ordered the books burned. On February 3, 1853, all copies went up in flames, with the exception of one kept for use by the Petersburg Censorial Committee.[21]

Although the *Dictionary* quickly disappeared from circulation, it became well known in progressive circles. Both volumes were found in the library of Nikolaj Alekseevič Nekrasov. In 1847 Herzen took the second volume with him to Paris where he showed it to Bakunin and his other *emigré* friends. The *Dictionary* was first quoted by Friedrich Engels in an article in 1871.[22]

---

[20] Semevskij, *Petraševskij i Petraševcy*, p. 60.
[21] "Cenzura v carstvovanii imperatora Nikolaja pervogo", *Russkaja starina*, 8 (August 1903), pp. 421-422.
[22] V. R. Lejkina-Svirskaja, "Revoljucionnaja praktika Petraševcev", *Istoričeskie zapiski*, XLVII (1954), p. 193.

Aside from the *Dictionary*, Petraševskij's writings were left in the form of rough drafts, sketches or remarks. In addition, there was his written testimony to the Investigating Commission charged with his affair following his arrest in April, 1849, but this document may not be thoroughly reliable as an index to Petraševskij's thoughts because of his obvious reasons under the circumstances for moderating any beliefs hostile to the regime.

Petraševskij seems to have carried into his adult years many of the sophomoric notions and petty rebellions of his Lyceum days. Time and again he seems to have interacted abrasively with people when a bit of mature concession would have accomplished much more. He was a dilettante, described by one of his Lyceum contemporaries as "a kind of intellectual premature child unable to imagine his actions with an intelligently created goal".[23] He read a great deal, but much of what he read was illconsumed. He did not always have strong convictions, but once Petraševskij decided upon a course of action his will was unshakable. Semenov described him as "an excellent type of innate agitator".[24] Petraševskij loved propaganda and agitational activity and tried to promote them on all levels of society.

The *Petraševec* Fedor Nikolaevič L'vov portrayed Petraševskij as acting not from the inspiration of feeling, but from considerations of cold reason. Petraševskij often acted unselfishly, but when L'vov noted that such acts were emotional rather than reasonable, Petraševskij was insulted and took great pains to prove the opposite. He saw each fact of human activity as the consequence of an idea; he searched only for the nearest causes, ignoring the fact that many human words and actions have causes far removed. For Petraševskij, a most insignificant act could have a great significance. For example, a man spat because he had bad manners, because he had a cough, because he smoked tobacco too strong for his constitution, or because he wished to show contempt. When faced with the necessity of deciding which of these propositions had the strongest base, Petraševskij would most often decide that the act was intentional: the man spat to show contempt. A man of passion, Petraševskij selected the supposition which he liked at a given moment and raised it to a conviction upon which he began to act. As a result, he needlessly created bitter enemies and afterwards was always amazed at his own perspicacity.[25]

---

[23] Veselovskij, *op. cit.*, p. 453.
[24] Ščegolev, *op. cit.*, p. 46.
[25] Ščegolev, *op. cit.*, I, pp. 136-137.

In a letter which he wrote to Herzen and Ogarev in 1860, M. A. Bakunin charged that Petraševskij was guilty of hiding behind a mask of legalisms. Bakunin, who did not meet Petraševskij until after many years of labor in Siberia had tarnished the reformer's idealism, described Petraševskij as a 'sharp' lawyer, but not a revolutionary. Petraševskij was no open fighter, Bakunin wrote, because he was not equipped to be one. Bakunin called him a coward and claimed he intrigued, played dirty jokes on people, intentionally sowed discord and dared talk about dangerous subjects. Even in the heat of argument, Bakunin found it impossible to insult Petraševskij; he concluded that if there were a revolution tomorrow Petraševskij would be out in the crowd for a while, but the next day would fall in the mud and be forgotten.

Bakunin chided Petraševskij's love of justice and said he found him entirely out of step with the literary and political movements of the day. He rebuked Petraševskij for reading without coherent planning and for seizing "upon great bunches of various branches of knowledge" which made up his world view.[26] It is particularly upon these points, however, that Bakunin's judgment is faulty. Petraševskij was definitely attuned to the political events of his day and had knowledge of political events all over Russia. For example, the police informer Antonelli reported that Petraševskij had detailed knowledge of political affairs at Kiev University and knew exactly who held *avant garde* convictions among the student youth at the universities in Moscow and Kharkov.

Bakunin's account of Petraševskij's preoccupation with legalism seems at least partly corroborated by the unfavorable light in which Petraševskij appeared in the novel *Aleksej Slobodin*, written in 1873 by Aleksander Pal'm, a former *Petraševec*. Petraševskij appeared as Dmitrij Sergeevič, described by another character in the novel as a madman unable to give account of his acts. Dmitrij always seemed confused, but he knew how to cover his errors. He stood immovable on the ground of legality.

At least one observer reported a devious side to Petraševskij's character. Antonelli wrote that he was afraid to play cards with Petraševskij because he always used the card game to explore his opponent's character. He never played for relaxation, but once the game started he would not quit until he had exhausted every chance of winning. In Petraševskij's own words: "Once I decide to throw myself into some-

---

[26] Ščegolev, *op. cit.*, I, p. 133.

thing, I do it with my whole heart and soul until I have attained my goal." [27]

Mixail Vasil'evič Petraševskij was, except for his insistence upon legal means to a desired end, an almost classic rebel. Restricted by his mother, unpopular with his peers and his elders in school, an insurgent in his office, an iconoclast in society – his life's pattern and style up to the time of his arrest and even, to a degree, afterwards suggest that he probably could never have been other than the restless intellectual agitator he was.

[27] Desnitskij, I, p. 404.

II

PETRAŠEVSKIJ AND FOURIERISM

As Alexander Herzen had done before him, Petraševskij looked to socialism for ways to correct the inequality, injustice, and repression which he found in the Russia of the 1840s; like Herzen, he believed that socialism constituted the most effective form of protest. Unlike Herzen, however, Petraševskij became passionately obsessed with the socialistic concepts of the Frenchman, François Marie Charles Fourier (1772-1837). To Petraševskij Fourierism was much more than just another ideology; it was a religion. He long remembered the experience of first hearing the words of Fourier as being a moment of rebirth in life for him. "If I had had the opportunity", Petraševskij recalled, "I would have made a unique divinity of him."[1]

Petraševskij's interpretation of Fourierism was based on the doctrine of association, a principle which was basic to all of Fourier's work. Fourier believed that the combined action of a group of individuals was superior to the actions of separate individuals; in isolation, he believed, one became unproductive. Therefore, the primary unit of the new social structure would have to be the phalanstery, the communal dwelling place of a number of members. Several phalansteries would be associated into a phalanx. From this center, the strength of the principle of association was to radiate throughout the society.

Also basic to his doctrine was Fourier's lack of interest in changing human nature; he did not believe, as the Saint-Simonians did, that such a change was necessary to social reform. Fourier took man as he understood him to be and hoped to render him happy by finding outlets for all his passions. The Jacobins embodied all that Fourier opposed because in their 'Republic of Virtue' they envisioned a utopia to which only the strictly conforming could be admitted. The key to the Jacobin ideal was that the Jacobins themselves would decide who was to be

[1] P. E. Ščegolev (ed.), *Petraševcy*, II (Moscow, 1927), p. 90.

admitted; they proposed to destroy all opposition. Fourier's experience in the French Revolution, and especially the Lyons uprising – in which he lost his personal fortune and narrowly escaped being executed – set him squarely against the use of violence in enforcing conformity.

In his first book, *Théorie des quatre mouvements et des destinées générales* (1808), Fourier called for a denial of all past philosophical and ethical schools, an *écarte absolu*. Furthermore, society could not remain static: in an unchanging social milieu man would wither on the vine. Society must advance, he said, through sixteen epochs until all men reached a state of harmony. There was to be a series of cycles, each one on a higher plane than the previous one. If followed to its logical conclusion, this upward spiral would end in a Kingdom of Heaven on earth.[2] The founder of the new society and ultimate savior of mankind, Fourier prophesied, would be an inventor or a carpenter.

The state of universal harmony toward which Fourier's cycles of social development were directed could be reached only when men were completely free in the expression of their passions. Fourier defined twelve basic human passions and divided them into three categories. First, there were the five material passions, the active senses of taste (*goût*), touch (*toucher*), smell (*ororat*), sight (*vue*) and hearing (*ouie*). Then there were the four passions of sociability, which served as means of communication among people and joined them together in groups: friendship (*amitié*), ambition (*ambition*), love (*amour*) and parenthood (*parenté*).

Finally, Fourier wrote, there were the three distributive passions: the passion for making arrangements (*passion composite*), from which one got a sense of satisfaction in making arrangements for others; the passion of intrigue (*passion cabaliste*), by which he explained people's fondness for making contracts and their interest in intrigues; the passion of variety (*passion papillone*), the 'butterfly passion', which was the most important of the twelve because it was an instrument of freedom.[3] The passion of variety could only be satisfied in a society that allowed for frequent changes of occupations and loves. When all twelve passions could be freely exercised, then man's strongest passion, harmony, could be realized.

Petraševskij adopted wholeheartedly Fourier's view that the sole reason for man's existence on earth is his realization of his own happi-

---

[2] Charles Fourier, *Œuvres complètes de Charles Fourier*, VI, second edition (Paris, 1841-1845), p. 418.

ness, a goal which he achieves only after all evil has been destroyed. Evil, Fourier instructed his readers, is not the result of social or humanistic relationships. It is not produced by the commission of an evil act for the sake of the act, but by permitting a small evil act to be committed as a means toward some greater good, a permission that violates man's harmony with his environment. The willfulness of the individual personality is thus responsible for the development of evil.

Fourier saw the domination of some men by others as a violation of natural harmony. Such inequality in human relationships occurs, he wrote, because people are divided into classes, each of which has its own interests at heart and attempts to appropriate for itself the welfare that rightfully belongs to all of humanity. Furthermore, a great deal of disharmony is created by the concept of private property, which breeds a spirit of exclusiveness in society. The resulting competition puts members of society against one another, each man searching independently for his happiness and often creating his own prosperity upon the failures of others. The concept of mutual aid (*vzaimnaja pomošč'*), a keystone in the Russian interpretation of Fourierism, grew from Fourier's belief that the happiness of man can be realized only when all members of society understand the foolishness of individual and class competition and participate in helping one another.

This universal participation in the construction of a better society, Petraševskij averred, demanded association. People must agree to live in communal units, from which any person could withdraw at will. The unit, or phalanstery, would allow freedom of worship. All work would be voluntary and based upon the individual's ability, and all means of production would be community-owned. Each worker would have an assigned role in society. He would belong to a certain series or category of labor, and the work he did within that category would satisfy the three distributive passions, for making arrangements, for intrigue and for variety. Each individual could engage in forty or fifty branches of industry; he could pursue a plurality of groups and functions. In this way his ego would be absorbed in myriad attachments, and the social spirit of the individual and the mass would unite.

Petraševskij accepted Fourier's premise that a sound economic structure was essential to the new society. From economic disorder sprang social disorder. The political structure of a society developed from its economic and social forces. Therefore, the phalanx would not be authentic if it were not an economic as well as a social grouping. Directing the economic progress of each phalanx would be a purely consultative administration which would organize the labor series but which would have no authority over the means of production nor the power to make community regulations. This 'economic regime' would have no status outside its own phalanx. Within the phalanx, the regime would be authorized only to keep production records, see to the efficiency of the local economy, and assure the complete satisfaction of the needs and desires of the individual.[3]

To Fourier, the most important function of the phalanx was agricultural. If possible, each phalanx was to be self-sufficient, although both Fourier and Petraševskij believed in free trade and limited competition among phalanxes. The idea of socialistic competition, they agreed, would be good for the whole economy and would help assure the filling of each consumer's needs, regardless of differences in local productions. The phalanxes would participate in a harmonious open market, thus eliminating the need for a commercial middle class. On the other hand, Fourier stated, the phalanxes would cooperate in the establishment of rural banks which would finance the clearing of lands and new construction. Actually, by 1840, the time of Petraševskij's first acquaintance with Fourierism, over 1,000 small rural banks and about 100 mutual aid and savings banks had already been established in Russia, though certainly not as any result of Fourier's socialist teachings.[4]

In his interpretation of Fourierism, Petraševskij defended his mentor's notions of marital and sexual morality. Free love, Petraševskij argued, was necessary to the free and full development of the individual. The ultimate responsibility of each person must be the uninhibited development of his own abilities. While opposing all moralistic religious dogma on the grounds that dogma blinds men to truth, Petraševskij wrote, "Those who call Fourier's system immoral clearly show that they do not comprehend his system."[5] Even so, Petraševskij's propaganda on free love was considerably subdued in comparison to Fourier's original hypothesis and did not develop Fourier's elaborate detail for free love in the phalanstery.[6]

Petraševskij also accepted with some modification Fourier's notions concerning marriage. Fourier insisted that all was false and immoral in marriage, that not love but economic considerations were the bases for

---

[3] Fourier, *op. cit.*, p. 90.
[4] Sergei Pushkarev, *The Emergence of Modern Russia, 1801-1917*, trans. Robert H. McNeal and Tova Yedlin (New York, 1963), p. 42.
[5] V. A. Desnitskij (ed.), *Delo Petraševcev*, I (Moscow, 1937), p. 82.
[6] I. I. Zil'berfarb, *Social'naja filosofija Šarlja Fur'e i ee mesto v istorii socialisti-českoj mysli pervoj poloviny XIX veka* (Moscow, 1964), p. 347.

most marriages, and that for most people monogamy was evil. The average person, Fourier argued, was naturally polygamous and social repression of this nature left him unfulfilled. Reason in such matters should be replaced by passion. The family unit should be replaced by the phalanstery. In each phalanstery would live 810 men and 810 women, with each individual representing a different combination of passions. In a group of 1,620 people, there should be enough combinations of passions to satisfy even the most bizarre inclination.

Education was as important to Fourier's concept of the evolution of humanity as we have already seen it was to Petraševskij's. By lifting the individual out of the state of confusion into which he was born, Fourier suggested, education helped him evolve until he reached the final state of true harmony. Petraševskij agreed, adding that education and schools should be directly related to man's teleological ends. He believed in education for the entire people, "to free their egos from the inclination toward a coarse sensuality; this can be changed through a correct understanding of what their true capabilities are." [7] Petraševskij felt that the more educated the people were, the less chance there was for criminality in society. In terms of total social reform, it was the basic problem of the ignorant masses that needed attention in Russia. A wide range of knowledge had to be spread among the lower classes as well as among the upper classes. A new Fourierist society must not make the mistake of the Decembrists by failing to educate all levels of society in the new ideology. Fourierism itself, he reasoned, would play an important role in eradicating ignorance in Russia. [8]

Petraševskij saw, however, that Russia was not ready for any quick, drastic changes in education. Peter the Great had erred more than a century before in bringing in changes too quickly. Enlightenment of the masses was necessary before any drastic changes in the education system could take place. A prerequisite was the abolition of press censorship, since prior censorship was incompatible with the encouragement of enlightenment. But after elaborating upon Fourier's call for educational reform, Petraševskij was apparently unable to spell out in practical terms how such reform could be brought about, other than to suggest hopefully that in the course of social evolution, Russian schools would come to produce students with a strong sense of citizenship and the responsibility for helping others.

[7]   V. E. Evgrafov (ed.), *Filosofskie i obščestvenno-političeskie proizvedenija Petraševcev* (Moscow, 1953), p. 117.
[8]   Desnitskij, *op. cit.*, I, p. 73.

Although Petraševskij was greatly inspired by Fourier's socialist system, he was by no means able to integrate Fourierism *in toto* into his dream of turning Russia into a free, happy society. For example, he was unable to accept the Frenchman's doctrine of the nature of the universe and the transmigration of souls, which was based to a large extent upon Newton's idea that objects seek out other objects because of a mutual attraction. He also had no use for Fourier's suggestion of a sexual relationship between planets.

Petraševskij was quick to see the impracticability in Russia of Fourier's notions of state and government. Fourier felt that under certain circumstances it would be convenient to have the government participate in social reform. While contributing, it would transform itself into part of the system. The state could function as intermediary during the period when the phalansteries were being established. If it were purged of unscrupulous politicians who might make use of the reform for their own ends, the government could regulate commerce and protect the agriculturists against the greedy industrialists. Eventually the transition period would be past and the state would wither away of its own accord.

Petraševskij was not so naive as to believe that Nicholas I would show any interest in the introduction of Fourierism into Russia, although one of the *Petraševcy*, N. S. Kaškin, seemed to think it was possible. After all, there was an inordinate gap between the political conditions of France and Russia. In France one could be a socialist openly in the 1840s; Louis Blanc was a member of the Provisional Government in 1848. In Russia, dissemination of even the most innocuous socialist propaganda was illegal. At the very mention of the word socialism, the Tsar jumped to the conclusion that an overthrow of his government was imminent. Petraševskij was aware that openly spreading new ideas in Russia was nearly impossible because "anything that was new would be thought of as being immoral and illegal."[9]

Despite the difficulties he found in trying to apply Fourierism to the whole cloth of Russian life, Petraševskij was unendingly fascinated with Fourier's ideas. He was so fascinated, in fact, that he decided in 1847 to built a phalanstery among his own peasants. He owned a hamlet of seven houses situated on marshy land and at the edge of a large wood near St. Petersburg. The hamlet was inhabited by forty serfs, their wives and their children. Living was difficult for them, for although they had enough land, raising cattle was hard, the farming implements were primitive, and the houses were in poor repair.

[9] Evgrafov, *op. cit.*, p. 322.

When the bailiff of the hamlet came to him for authorization to cut wood for repairs, Petraševskij proposed that the peasants leave the unhealthy marsh and build a vast commune in the forest for their families. Each family, he explained, would have a separate apartment, but the kitchen and the room set aside for the winter days when there was no outside work would be communal. There would also be a large modern outhouse and a tool shed. Petraševskij offered to bear the expense.

Petraševskij developed at length the advantages of such an association, but the bailiff remained unconvinced. The peasants would not like it, the bailiff warned; they did not understand change and they resented it.

Undaunted, Petraševskij ordered the work begun, hoping that when the peasants had finished, they would appreciate the advantages of the new organization. The building progressed rapidly. Petraševskij bought new household equipment and improved farming implements. He was frequently on hand with explanations and advice for the future phalansterians. By Christmas, 1847, all was ready.

Shortly after New Year's Day, 1848, one of the *Petraševcy*, Zotov, asked Petraševskij about his phalanstery. Petraševskij confessed that on the day of the inauguration of his project, he had gone to the forest and found the commune in ruins. In the night, the peasants had burned it to the ground.

"There was so much grief in his voice", Zotov said later, "that it was made impossible for me even to laugh while learning about the catastrophe of the project of the Great Lord of socialist tendencies."[10]

Despite the failure of what was to be the first Russian experiment in Fourierism, Petraševskij had no thought of renouncing the French socialist's ideology. To the contrary, he was convinced that Russia where the peasants had known the collective *mir*, or *obščina*, for centuries was more prepared to benefit from Fourierism than was western Europe, where the peasant was traditionally more individualized. At the time of his arrest in 1849, Petraševskij was still ordering his interpretation of Fourierism and planning means by which it could be brought to fruition in Russia.

---

[10] V. I. Semevskij, *Sobranie sočinenij: M. V. Butaševič-Petraševskij i Petraševcy*, ed. V. V. Vodovozov, II (Moscow, 1922), pp. 174-176; George Sourine, *Le Fourierisme en Russie* (Paris, 1936), pp. 58-59.

III

PETRAŠEVSKIJ'S SOCIAL CRITIQUE
AND ORGANIZATION FOR SOCIAL CHANGE

Petraševskij's fixation upon France as an almost utopian model for social and political reform in Russia has already been noted. He came to regard Republican France as having developed one of history's best governmental forms. The National Convention, he felt, gave the people at large the best opportunity for representation, and the Declaration of the Rights of Man of 1789 seemed to him a superior document of revolutionary civil and human rights. He noted, according to *The Pocket Dictionary of Foreign Words,* that Russia in the 1840s had not even developed a meaningful concept of civil rights, much less enshrined it in a constitution.

On the other hand, Petraševskij was also influenced by Alexis de Tocqueville's history of France under the Ancient Regime. Tocqueville had written: "The political men of letters of the eighteenth century think it suitable to substitute simple, elementary rules, inspired by reason and natural law, for the complicated and traditional customs which rule the society of their time." [1] Sensing the parallels which could be drawn between eighteenth-century France and his contemporary Russia, Petraševskij began to envision for his own country a political system based on reason, natural law and a return to a more simplified structure.

Petraševskij favored a federative political structure for Russia, feeling that this form would bring the people political freedom as well as social reform. Among the repressive policies of Nicholas I was the use of armed force to keep the provinces from breaking away to form independent states. Although his federative concepts were only poorly developed, Petraševskij expressed the hope that in the future the provinces would achieve the same relationship to the central government that the individual states had achieved with the federal government in the United States, and that the use of force to keep Russia in one piece

---

[1] Alexis de Tocqueville, *L'Ancien régime* (Paris, 1952), p. 194.

would then be unnecessary.[2] Enlarging his vision somewhat, Petraševskij also suggested that the nations of the world should develop an interrelationship similar to that of the several United States. An ideal international order, he believed, should be based on the principle of nationality, with no nation being allowed to enlarge itself at the expense of its neighbors. In such an order warfare would be obsolete; in the new world, Petraševskij declared, armies would have no place.[3]

The state, in Petraševskij's view, existed only to attend to the welfare of the people,[4] and should be guided in this regard by natural law. The state was no more than any other social organization; it was empowered only to provide man with the means for the satisfaction of the various needs of his character. Consequently, the state had to conform to the principle of legality. Laws, created rationally by men for the regulation of man in society, must derive from the people and must be codified.

Democracy, to Petraševskij, was the form of government which would be most in harmony with human nature. He suggested that mass participation by the people is necessary for the success of any government, since such participation would ensure the government's dedication to the general welfare. A pure democracy would be impractical, however, so Petraševskij admitted the legitimacy of indirect representation in the form of a legislature.

He qualified his democratic ideal still further by contending that some are born to rule while others are born to serve. The rulers would rise out of the 'intellectual aristocracy' (*umstvennaja aristokratija*) as the result of elections in which only the best qualified would be chosen. In time, the government would be styled an elective or democratic oligarchy.[5] Of course, all citizens would be guaranteed civil and personal rights in Petraševskij's new society. He believed that a kind of 'natural justice' would ensure the safety of all citizens. But he did not believe in a natural equality among men; the more talented would definitely be favored, a social factor which Petraševskij adopted from Plato and Fourier, while the political freedom of the masses would be ensured by a form of political toleration similar to the spirit of toleration which he found described in Jeremy Bentham's discussion of English political life.

[2] V. I. Semevskij, *Sobranie sočinenij: M. V. Butaševič-Petraševskij i Petraševcy*, ed. V. V. Vodovozov, II (Moscow, 1922), p. 138.
[3] George Sourine, *Le Fourierisme en Russie* (Paris, 1936), p. 32.
[4] V. E. Evgrafov (ed.), *Filosofskie i obščestvenno-političeskie proizvedenija Petraševcev* (Moscow, 1953), p. 118.
[5] Evgrafov, *op. cit.*, p. 280.

While admiring the United States Constitution and the French Constitution of 1791 as nearly perfect documents, Petraševskij also found inspiration in Russia's own past. He found in the Assembly of the Land (*Zemskij sobor*), which had last met in the seventeenth century, a precedent for his scheme of a National Assembly in Russia; although none of his proposals was based directly upon the Assembly of the Land, he nevertheless was impressed by the fact that it represented a significant section of the population beyond the court and governing circles.

The National Assembly of Petraševskij's vision would be invested with the supreme power of the nation.[6] It would have multiple responsibilities: it would deliberate laws, maintain the army, make war and peace, supervise public education, and at all times serve as an honest representative of the people.[7] Petraševskij hoped that through universal suffrage the will of the people would be carried out by the Assembly as a whole. He made no plans for a national executive officer, apparently being determined that no one man should gain dictatorial power.

Petraševskij's Assembly would deliberate in an atmosphere of free debate. With parliamentary struggle as its medium and the people's best interests as its selfless motivation, the Assembly would automatically be the ideal governing body. With a not unwonted degree of impracticality, however, Petraševskij apparently took no notice of the possibility that special interests might influence the delegates' deliberations, for he made no allowances for it.

Despite the fervor of his conviction that serfdom was evil and inhumane and must be rooted out of Russian society as soon as possible, Petraševskij gave first priority in his plans to court reform. He stated that just as political debate must be free and unencumbered, so the judicial system must be completely removed from the control of special interests. All cases should be tried publicly by jury and the accused should have the right to counsel.[8] Jury trial was at the heart of his plan for judicial reform, for Petraševskij felt that a jury represented the people and that the people would never let injustice occur because they were free.

Petraševskij suffered no illusions about the gap separating his reasonably defined ideal state from the contemporary political reality in Russia. In fact, he was convinced that everything in Russia was rotten. He enjoyed telling amusing stories that depicted Nicholas I as a fool,

[6] V. A. Desnitskij (ed.), *Delo Petraševcev*, III (Moscow, 1951), p. 383.
[7] Desnitskij, *op. cit.*, III, p. 383.
[8] Evgrafov, p. 198.

but he felt that the Tsar was crippled by a spiritual sickness which made him dangerous, and that each day Nicholas' "course of action became more unbearable and that more and more he was coming to resemble Pavel I".[9]

Petraševskij's most powerful weapon against the regime was the *Dictionary*, into which he packed the most acid criticism of social and political conditions in Russia. Indeed, it would be impossible to find in that august work one word of praise for any Russian institution. In one way or another, almost all of Petraševskij's entries touch on the problems of man in relation to the society in which he lives. In a cleverly designed definition of a 'normal' condition (*normal'noe sostojanie*), Petraševskij describes Russian society as it would be if his political ideal were put into effect. A 'normal' state of affairs should be a society in which all men strive for a better existence. Thus it is perfectly 'normal' for each man to want his children to have a better education than he had. At least the minimum necessities of life must be provided. In society a 'normal' condition permits each member the means to satisfy his needs in proportion to his wants. The role of the individual, however, must be severely restricted so that his pursuit of his wants does not disturb the harmony of social relationships. He must be a cog in a machine.[10] Only by behaving in this way can a man contribute to the 'normal' functioning of his society.

In Russia, according to Petraševskij, the way toward 'normalcy' was blocked by the 'obscurantists'. Obscurantism, which repressed democratic ideals, was the work of those reactionary bureaucrats and church officials who held the reigns of authority. They kept the masses in ignorance about those affairs in which the public had every right to be interested. To the obscurantists, Petraševskij charged, it was more respectable to rule slaves and cretins than to rule real people endowed with consciousnesses. They believed in the moral destruction of the personality – in short, the ultimate dehumanizing of the soul. 'Sometimes', Petraševskij wrote, 'they were successful in killing in their victims any impulse toward thinking and the investigation of nature.'[11]

Among the obscurantists he attacked were leaders of the Orthodox faith. Petraševskij termed himself an atheist because he stood against organized religion's encroachments on society. He was favorably impressed, however, with the New Christianity of the Frenchman Saint-

---

[9]   Semevskij, *Petraševskis i Petraševcy*, p. 146.
[10] Evgrafov, *op. cit.*, p. 238.
[11] Evgrafov, *op. cit.*, p. 259.

Simon, in which religion is subordinated to the social law of organic development. Saint-Simon's progressive (*novateur*) would break with organized religion and establish a new clergy made up of the most talented people in society.[12] Toward the end of developing harmonious social relationships, Petraševskij agreed with Saint-Simon's theory of the association of all Christians. But in Russia, he felt, the obscurantist church hierarchy formed an effective part of the blockade against progress.

The obscurantist hindered the teaching of true Christianity; indeed, he hindered all education. He used his own education, Petraševskij wrote, to keep education from others. With monstrous irony, Petraševskij commented:

There is none of this in Russia. Thanks to the wisdom of our government which long ago chased out the Jesuits, the great influence of obscurantism has been considerably weakened in comparison with the other governments of Europe, as for example, Austria.[13]

The obscurantists and Petraševskij were mortal enemies. He wished to teach Fourierism in Russia that there might result a more educated public opinion. The obscurantist was violently opposed to the spreading of ideas by any means. The obscurantist, Petraševskij charged:

was an enemy of any publicity in the administration of Justice, as well as in society as a whole ... He liked secrecy, privilege, separation and he liked to keep the classes of the people hostile to each other ... It was impossible or disadvantageous for him to recognize the possibility of peaceful relationships among human beings and the assertion on the earth of the brotherhood of man.[14]

A recurring theme in Petraševskij's characterization of the world is man's inhumanity to man. As far as he was concerned, the most nefarious miscreancy in Russia was serfdom, and he attacked it at every opportunity, usually on humanitarian rather than economic grounds.

In discussing the plight of the Russian serf in his *Dictionary* entries, Petraševskij was prudent enough to avoid using the Russian terms 'serf' and 'serfdom'. Instead, he seized upon the institution of Negro slavery in the western world as a contemporary analogy to serfdom. Both the Negro and – by implication – the serf were in their inferior positions because of the spiritual isolation artificially imposed on them by the ruling classes. This spiritual isolation had the effect over many

---

12 Claude Henri de Saint-Simon, *Nouveau Christianisme* (Paris, 1832), p. 20.
13 Evgrafov, *op. cit.*, p. 261.
14 Evgrafov, *op. cit.*, p. 261.

generations of dehumanizing the serf and the Negro; as a result of their exploitation by their rulers, Petraševskij stated, they had lost all traces of intelligence. They were reduced to the level of animals. Petraševskij reinforced this point in another *Dictionary* entry when he defined *odaliska*, the Turkish word for prostitute, as a woman who had lost all human characteristics and had reverted to the animal level because she had been 'exploited'.[15] The only means by which these dehumanized spirits could be brought back into the civilized world, he concluded, was education.

Veiling his implications in Aesopic language, Petraševskij recalled for the *Dictionary's* readers the situation of the Negroes on Santo Domingo in the early nineteenth century. The black former slaves had constructed a republican form of government by borrowing the institutions of their 'civilized' masters. For Petraševskij, the self-rule of the ex-slaves in Haiti was shining proof that the oppressed had the talent, if given a chance, to be just as 'civilized' as the oppressor.

Petraševskij referred to the Negro government of Liberia as another example of what Negroes could do if they had their freedom. Concluding his exposition of the evils of slavery and the potential of free men, he asked, "Why, then, if given a chance, could not the Russian serf help construct a more viable social order in Russia?"[16]

Last in Petraševskij's established order of important reforms was the reform of censorship procedures. He advised caution in this area because too hasty reform might have a deleterious effect upon the people: only confusion would result from the establishment of wholesale license for anyone to write anything he pleased. Despite his apparent radicalism, Petraševskij feared unbridled freedom; he fully realized the dangers inherent in the freeing of the oppressed 'dark people' (*čern'*). Released suddenly from slavery, they might vent generations of frustration upon the upper classes in disastrous civil war. Petraševskij hoped that, instead, social reform would follow an orderly process from court reform through legal emancipation of the serfs and so to censorship reform, each stage being a natural outgrowth of its predecessor.

Where would the initiative for reform come from? Ideally, Petraševskij noted, it should come from the Senate. However, he held a low opinion of the Senate as an institution. In his view, there were at the time only a few senators who were 'enlightened' enough to lend a

---

15 Evgrafov, *op. cit.*, p. 272.
16 Evgrafov, *op. cit.*, p. 208.

sympathetic hearing to his ideas.[17] The senators served not to meet the needs of the people, Petraševskij had decided, but for the sake of their own personal prestige.

Consequently, he hoped that the impetus for reform would come from the 'intellectual aristocracy', which included merchants, teachers, doctors, druggists, priests, and retired poor bureaucrats.[18] He envisioned such intellectuals uniting around a leader, who could then successfully present himself to the Senate as representing significant political power. Even as he devised this rather hazy plan, Petraševskij was aware that the Tsar would brook no such opposition. So all notions of reform had to be carefully but discreetly nurtured among the intellectual aristocracy until proposals could be made openly. In the meantime, intellectuals should bide their time by "unconditionally accepting every measure of the government which furthers a greater degree of stabilization of the means of preserving personal safety and civic freedom".[19] Petraševskij's writings do not make clear what the intellectual aristocracy was to do if the regime decided to take repressive measures against it. A form of passive resistance is implied. Petraševskij's greatest fear was that if the government were provoked and aroused, it would crush the opposition and all his reform plans.

The task of defining Petraševskij's views on social change must ultimately remain uncompleted because Petraševskij took few pains himself to define them carefully. He does not denounce revolution as a means to social reform, and his writings indicate his constant awareness of the possibility that the 'dark people' might revolt. But although his contemporary, Alexander Herzen, believed him a revolutionary[20] and the modern Soviet historian Vera Romanovna Lejkina-Svirskaja calls him a "revolutionary democrat",[21] Petraševskij must not be thought of as a latter-day Pugačev leading a spontaneous revolt of the peasants. While he was not unshakably opposed to revolution, he hoped it could be averted. He felt that every other possible means to reform had to be exhausted before revolution should even be seriously discussed. He found much more appealing as an alternative to violent uprising an example set by the speech of Count Mirabeau before the French Na-

---

[17] Semevskij, *Petraševskij i Petraševcy*, p. 145.
[18] Semevskij, *op. cit.*, II, p. 186.
[19] Evgrafov, *op. cit.*, p. 296.
[20] A. Herzen, "Petrashevsky", *Revue politique et littéraire (Revue bleue)*, XLVI (November 1908), p. 387.
[21] V. R. Lejkina-Svirskaja, "Revoljucionnaja praktika Petraševcev", *Istoričeskie zapiski*, XLVII (1954), pp. 181-223.

tional Assembly in 1789. Mirabeau had convinced his fellow nobles to give up their feudal rights. As Petraševskij recounted the incident, Mirabeau appealed to the nobility to "repress their egotistical feelings and renounce, for the sake of others, certain grievous rights and privileges".[22] There was no reason why the Russian gentry could not do the same, he concluded, yielding freely those rights which might otherwise be the prize of revolution.

Petraševskij treats at great length the idea of reform by example. According to his *Dictionary* entries, the 'innovators' (*novatory*), those who contributed to the arts and sciences, were essential to social transformation. An invention such as Robert Fulton's steamboat was quite important because it transported people and forced them to change their habits. Petraševskij alluded to Jesus Christ as the greatest 'innovator' in history because his death by crucifixion and the faith built upon it were held up to mankind as means to redemption.[23] Although he was not a Christian, Petraševskij found in Jesus Christ an excellent example of the powers of the innovator in society.

However, Petraševskij was quick to point out the difference between the 'innovator' and the 'revolutionary'. The concept of innovation was centered in the idea of reform; it really meant "the transformation of form and not of essence".[24] Innovation was carried out in order to bring its subject to a 'normal' state. In this striving for 'normalcy' (the way society should be if it were allowed to develop naturally and without repression of any of its members), social change should come without violence. In Petraševskij's vision of change, there is at all times a consciousness of legality implicit in the means to change in society. In this kind of theoretical discussion, Petraševskij rejects revolution, primarily because he believes it should be unnecessary. He points for illustration to the French Revolution of 1789, suggesting that it could have been an orderly, peaceful social transformation if Louis XVI had supported the sensible decisions of the National Assembly. Russia, he concludes, should benefit from France's mistakes.

In February 1848, scarcely two months after his peasants had burned their phalanstery, Petraševskij was again theorizing enthusiastically about political reform. He presented a tract entitled "On the means of increasing the value of gentry or populated estates" to the

---

[22]   Evgrafov, *op. cit.*, p. 68.
[23]   Evgrafov, *op. cit.*, p. 250.
[24]   Evgrafov, *op. cit.*, p. 197.

Assembly of the Gentry in St. Petersburg.[25] The tract did not call for an absolute abolition of serfdom, but for a gradual evolution toward a more balanced society. Petraševskij saw as the chief obstacle to reform the gentry's sole right of ownership to populated lands.

The allotment of land to one class only has contributed to the small amount of capital available; this is reflected in industry, the non-development of credit and the appreciable lack of places and establishments for its own development; the uncertainty in the future which the landowners faced is based on decisions made in the past ten years.[26]

In a nine-point plan, the tract called for changes in land ownership policies. Petraševskij proposed that merchants acquire land and be granted certain gentry rights on the condition that they assume responsibility for the peasants living on the land. If this scheme were carefully executed, merchants would eventually control gentry lands worth up to 500 million rubles.

In order to speed up the acquisition process, the merchants would be allowed to make loans to the gentry. Land banks and credit establishments would be set up. Interest rates would be lowered. Petraševskij proposed that agricultural produce be accepted as credit deposit, an idea he borrowed from the French. He wanted savings accounts opened for rural priests to give them a sense of participation in the country's development. He saw the need for improvements in the legal system to help stabilize prices of landed estates. In all, Petraševskij felt, the strengthening of credit would help cement a feeling of trust among people.

In official circles, Petraševskij's plan was received with great distaste. The leader (predvoditel') of the Petersburg provincial gentry immediately turned over his copy of the plan to the Tsar in an attempt to block discussion of it among the gentry. Nicholas ordered a ban on public and private discussion of the proposal. Petraševskij himself was expressly forbidden to mention any details of the plan openly. According to Semevskij, the Tsar "called the author a madman because he wanted to upset the existing order of things".[27]

Petraševskij distributed more than 200 lithographed copies of his tract, and several gentry landowners in Petersburg, Jamburgskij, and

[25] "O sposobax uveličenija cennosti dvorjanskix ili naselennyx imenij", P. E. Ščegolev (ed.), Petraševcy, II (Moscow, 1927), pp. 82-84.
[26] "O sposobax uveličenija . . ."
[27] Semevskij, Petraševskij i Petraševcy, pp. 111-112.

Carskosel'skij districts (*uezdy*) formed committees to study his proposals and make recommendations. But the Ministry of Internal Affairs saw in the plan's call for a basic change in the class structure of the country a seriously subversive act and abruptly terminated the gentry committees.

Interest in Petraševskij's plan was markedly lower among gentry living farther from St. Petersburg. Vladimir Ivanovič Kajdanov, a *Petraševec* who was living at the time in Jaroslav province, argued that it would be better if populated land prices depreciated, forcing the government to take action to keep the estates from going bankrupt. At the same time, Kajdanov hoped, the government would have to grapple with the problem of what to do about the serfs. Kajdanov also scorned Petraševskij's plan for merchant acquisition of gentry lands, contending that the merchants would treat the serfs even worse than did the present owners.[28] This latter opinion was supported generally by landowners in other provinces.

Petraševskij had much earlier realized that for the moment the ballot was his most potent weapon against Nicholas' bureaucratic regime. So shortly after the release of his tract "On the means of increasing the value of gentry or populated estates", he presented himself as candidate for the posts of secretary in the Gentry Assembly (*dvorjanskoe sobranie*) and secretary in the St. Petersburg Town Council (*Petersburgskaja gorodskaja duma*). He 'campaigned' by sending out notes to the gentry (*zapiski k dvorjanam*) in which he discussed the importance of elections. He was defeated, probably, according to Semevskij, because the merchant electorate did not understand a word of the argument in the notes.[29] But his failure at the polls, while underscoring the difficulties he faced in disseminating his democratic ideals, is not as important as the precedent he set in attempting to disseminate such ideals at all.

Petraševskij's election defeat did not in the least dampen his enthusiasm for reform. He went on to devise a scheme entitled "A project for the emancipation of the serfs". In the preface to this "project", Petraševskij offered the judgment that the many previous emancipation plans were unsatisfactory because they were too hastily drawn,[30] and because each reflected the interests of the author's social class. Petra-

---

[28] Semevskij, *op. cit.*, II, p. 114.
[29] Semevskij, *op. cit.*, II, p. 96.
[30] "Proekt osvoboždenija krest'jan", Evgrafov, *op. cit.*, pp. 359-364. This article also appears in Semevskij, "Petraševcy i krest'janskij vopros", *Velikaja reforma*, III (Moscow, 1911), pp. 205-220.

ševskij advocated the "unconditional freeing of the serfs with that land which had been worked by them".[31] While he is rather vague about the source of compensation to the nobles for the loss of their lands, Petraševskij is nevertheless adamant in his insistence that everyone in the world, farmer or not, was entitled to a plot of land which he could call his own. Petraševskij concluded with a very general statement that all the world's arable land should be divided equally among all the world's people. The article closes without offering a single suggestion as to how this massive reform might be carried out.

The essence of Petraševskij's ideas for social change, then, lies in basic reforms of the agencies of legislation and regulation, a loosening of traditional class restrictions, a land reform program which would include the collectivization of individually owned tracts into phalansteries and a considerable broadening of Russia's educational base. For many of these proposals his models were the legislation of the French National Assembly and French Fourierism; that much is clear. But what he so often leaves unclear are the means by which he would see these reforms accomplished.

---

[31] Evgrafov, *op. cit.*, p. 363.

IV

THE *PETRAŠEVCY*

On December 19, 1849, a Military-Civil court sitting in St. Petersburg found nineteen men guilty of subversive activities and sentenced them to be shot to death. These nineteen, who included Mixail Petraševskij, had been singled out, for one reason or another, from the more than 250 individuals who had had direct or indirect contact with Petraševskij, most of them through attendance at the discussion sessions held in his home on Friday evenings between January 1845, and April 1849. Those who attended Petraševskij's circle (*kružok*) or one of the circles organized by Petraševskij's colleagues, and who contributed through writings or speeches to the development of his plans for socialist reform in Russia, were known as the *Petraševcy*.

Twenty-five of the *Petraševcy* are worthy of particular mention, because it was they who attempted most seriously to grapple with the problems of political and social reform. They were bound together by a common concern for the welfare of the Russian lower classes and by a general admiration for western socialist literature, but often by little else. By and large they shared a gentry background and were members of the intelligentsia; most were young people with average incomes. Many had university educations, and all were convinced that some means must be found to bring change to Russia – even revolution, if it were necessary.

But among these twenty-five were many differences, too. Not all of them were from the St. Petersburg area; in fact, not all of them were Russians. A few had traveled outside the country and so had a more cosmopolitan view of social change than did the others. They were businessmen, military officers, students, and professors. They were distinguished by the widely varying limits to which they were prepared to go to bring reform to their country. Of the twenty-five, only one or two can be described as great thinkers who left their marks upon the nineteenth century.

Nikolaj Aleksandrovič Spešnev was the most widely traveled of the *Petraševcy*, and his knowledge of social conditions in the countries of western Europe commanded considerable respect in the eyes of his fellows. Spešnev, who served as the model for Dostoevskij's character Stavrogin in the novel *The Possessed*,[1] took an active role in all *Petraševcy* affairs, even going further than most in demanding the formation of a secret society.[2]

Spešnev was also one of the very few wealthy *Petraševcy*, the owner of an estate of about 500 serfs in Kursk province.[3] He had attended the Lyceum at Carskoe Selo but left in 1839 before completing the course. The next year, he fell in love with a neighbor's wife, a Pole, and persuaded her to leave her husband and two children to marry him and see Europe. After living in Helsinki for two years, they moved to Switzerland and then to Austria. Spešnev saw action in the *Sonderbund* war, taking part in the attack on Lucerne in 1843. In 1844, his wife died in Vienna, and Spešnev sent his two children to their uncle in Vitebsk and returned to visit a former Lyceum schoolmate in St. Petersburg. But later that year, he left again for Vienna and Dresden, where he scored great social successes in the Polish *emigré* circles to which his wife had belonged.

Spešnev made something of a scholarly name for himself between 1846 and 1849. He began with a study of the early history of the most successful of all secret societies, the Christians,[4] concentrating on their organizational structure while ignoring their ideology. Then in 1847, he undertook the study of socialism under the influence of the German 'Communist' Wilhelm Christian Weitling. He gained some prominence that year by contributing several articles on socialism to the *Revue Indépendente* in Paris.[5]

Spešnev returned to Russia, but maintained correspondence with Polish *emigré* circles in Paris, and particularly with the Polish journalist Edmund Chojecki, who had assisted the great Polish poet Adam Mickiewicz. Spešnev hoped to write a history of Russia which Chojecki would publish for him in Paris.[6] Spešnev later suggested that Chojecki's printing press be used to print anti-Tsarist propaganda for the

---

[1] K. V. Močul'skij, *Dostoevskij: Žizn' i tvorčestvo* (Paris, 1949), p. 109.
[2] *Bol'šaja sovetskaja ènciklopedija*, second edition, XXXII (1954), p. 590.
[3] V. I. Semevskij, *Sobranie sočinenij: M. V. Butaševich-Petraševskij i Petraševcy*, ed. V. V. Vodovozov, II (Moscow, 1922), p. 190.
[4] Močul'skij, *op. cit.*, p. 108.
[5] Pierre Leroux and George Sand were the editors.
[6] Semevskij, *Petraševskij i Petraševcy*, p. 193.

Petraševcy in Russia, a project in which he vainly tried to interest Russian writers who were disgusted with censorship.[7]

Shortly after returning to Russia, Spešnev took up residence in St. Petersburg, where he came again into contact with his old Lyceum friends. He was particularly interested to learn of the library of socialist literature that Petraševskij was collecting. In 1847, he joined Petraševskij's circle and submerged himself in the group's discussions of means of remedying the country's social ills.[8]

Sharing Spešnev's dissatisfaction with Fourierism was Rafail Aleksandrovič Černosvitov, who agreed that the Frenchman's philosophy was useless in the Russian context because it had nothing to say about revolution. Černosvitov was born in Jaroslav province of gentry stock. As a career military officer, he had taken part in the suppression of the Polish revolt of 1830; he had been captured and had lost a leg in a prison camp. Although he went into the reserve after being freed, he returned to active military life in the early 1840s and took part in suppressing the peasant revolts near the city of Perm'. Černosvitov and Spešnev, the vocal revolutionaries, were the only *Petraševcy* who had actually seen a revolt.

In 1842, Černosvitov left the army and went to Siberia to mine gold. He soon became a notable expert on Siberian affairs, and because of his gold mining success he wielded great political influence throughout the region.[9] In November, 1848, he visited St. Petersburg and became involved with the *Petraševcy*. In fact, the *Petraševcy* were much more interested in Černosvitov than he was in them; Petraševskij in particular was intrigued by his accounts of the conditions of the peasants in the area of the Urals. He was held in awe by the group at large because he had seen much more of the country than had any of them.

After two months, Černosvitov decided that the *Petraševcy* were nothing more than dilettantes, and so he returned to Siberia. Six months later, he was arrested in Tomsk in connection with the 'affair' of the *Petraševcy*.

As might be expected, there were those among the *Petraševcy* who could accept Fourierism but who could also rationalize revolution as a means of social reform. One of these was Konstantin Ivanovič Timkovskij, a graduate of the University of St. Petersburg and an expert

[7] V. R. Lejkina, *Petraševcy* (Moscow, 1924), p. 44.
[8] V. I. Semevskij, "Spešnev", *Ènciklopedičeskij slovar'*, XXXI (St. Petersburg, 1900), p. 316.
[9] Semevskij, *Petraševskij i Petraševcy*, p. 189.

in Oriental literature.[10] After naval service, Timkovskij had gone into the Ministry of Internal Affairs in Revel' (Tallinn). On a visit to St. Petersburg in November, 1848, he became acquainted with the Petraševcy. In the discussions he sided with Spešnev in favor of raising revolution. Upon his return to Revel' he attempted unsuccessfully to organize discussion groups there. Arrested in the spring of 1849, Timkovskij's brief period as a would-be revolutionary was immortalized in the character of Engineer Kirillov in Dostoevskij's novel *The Possessed*.[11]

Nikolaj Aleksandrovič Mombelli was another military officer who agreed with Petraševskij's interpretation of Fourierism. But Mombelli joined with other military officers among the Petraševcy who saw advantage in forming a secret society and working for the overthrow of the government. Mombelli, a native of Novozybkov, had already come under the scrutiny of his superiors when, in the winter of 1846-1847, he organized weekly discussion groups for his fellow officers.[12] Even though the discussion subjects were confined to literature, Mombelli's commanding officer heard that papers on social and scientific subjects were being read in the meetings and forbade their continuation.

Petraševskij heard of Mombelli's reputation as an army liberal and invited him to attend his 'Fridays'. Mombelli soon became an important member of the circle, but eventually his proposal of a society which would eschew violence and promote brotherhood among men on earth was rejected by the other Petraševcy. Mombelli was arrested along with the other members of the circle and sentenced to death.

Fedor Nikolaevič L'vov had entered the army while still in his teens. In the Pavlov Cadet Corps, he held the position of lecturer (*repetitor*) of chemistry.[13] Later, he was a member of Mombelli's discussion group and came to be known as a liberal by his fellow officers and his superiors. He shared Mombelli's disgust with conditions in the army, but, like Mombelli, was unable to make any effective protest. With Mombelli's help, he was admitted to the Petraševskij circle only shortly before being arrested in the spring of 1849.

Aleksandr Ivanovič Pal'm and Nikolaj Petrovič Grigor'ev were also labeled as liberal army officers. Pal'm began visiting the Petraševskij circle in 1847; presumably, he combined the discussion of reformist

---

[10] L. P. Grossman, *Dostoevskij* (Moscow, 1963), p. 107.
[11] Grossman, *op. cit.*, p. 107.
[12] Semevskij, *Petraševskij i Petraševcy*, p. 204.
[13] *Russkij biografičeskij slovar'*, X (1914), p. 790.

ideas with the gathering of material for a novel, for in 1873 he published *Aleksej Slobodin,* a fictionalized account of the *Petraševcy.*

Of all the officers who attended the Friday evening meetings, only
N. P. Grigor'ev advocated the formation of a secret society within the
army itself, either for purposes of reform or as an instrument of *coup
d'état.* Grigor'ev was not supported by the other *Petraševcy* in his
plans. When the regime cracked down on the circle, Grigor'ev was
among those sentenced to die.

Of those *Petraševcy* who displayed literary aspirations, the best
known is Fedor Mixajlovič Dostoevskij, who joined the Petraševskij
circle in 1847. Dostoevskij's place in the circle was never very great.
He was highly skeptical of Fourierism, believing that the Russian intellectual should seek the new Russian society not among the teachings
of western socialists but in the cultural and historical structure of the
Russian people, in such native institutions as the communes, "those
artels of circular security".[14]

Along with several other *Petraševcy*, Dostoevskij attended group
meetings in the home of the poet S. F. Durov, where he often read
aloud Puškin's poem "Solitude". One of those present recalled:

I can hear the delighted voice as it read through the concluding couplet:
"Will I see, friends, an unoppressed Russia?" When someone expressed
doubt at the possibility of the Emancipation by legal means, Dostoevskij
sharply objected that he didn't believe in any other means. Nevertheless,
according to the testimony of Pal'm when one time during a quarrel was
posed the question: "And if the emancipation of the peasant is impossible
except through a revolt?" then Dostoevskij with his usual passion answered,
"So let it be done through an uprising."[15]

Another of Dostoevskij's favorite readings in the company of the *Petraševcy* was the letter in which Belinskij chided Gogol', for his support
of the *status quo* in Nicholas' Russia.[16] Although he was not arrested
for his association with the *Petraševcy*, Dostoevskij was exiled for his
publication of the Belinskij letter.

The author Mixail Evgrafovič Saltykov stopped attending Petraševskij's Fridays in 1847, but his early novels continued to be a significant contribution to the socio-economic philosophy of the *Petraševcy*. In his first two novels, *Contradictions* (1846) and *A Confused*

---

[14] V. I. Semevskij, *Krest'janskij vopros v XVIII i v pervoj polovine XIX veka*, II
(St. Petersburg, 1888), p. 381.
[15] Semevskij, *Krest'janskij vopros*, II, p. 380.
[16] Močul'skij, *op. cit.*, p. 102.

Affair (1847), Saltykov played on the theme of the contradictions in life between theory and practice, intellect and feelings, idealism and realism, and the wealthy and the impoverished. Saltykov suggested that the reason for these contradictions was inequality (*neravenstvo*) which developed from the absolutist-based pyramidal structure of Russian society. These contradictions could only be resolved, he concluded, by working with the pyramid's base (the masses of people) and against its apex (the Tsar).[17]

No sooner had Saltykov's works begun appearing serialized in *Otečestvennye zapiski* than he came under the scrutiny of a special censorship committee, appointed by the Tsar and chaired by Admiral Aleksandr Sergeevič Menšikov, which was charged with ferreting out ideas that had drifted into Russia from western Europe.[18] At the time, Saltykov was employed in the Ministry of War. On the basis of the Menšikov committee's report, Nicholas I ordered Saltykov's superior, Minister of War A. I. Černyšev, to conduct a careful investigation of the whole affair. As a result of his investigation, Černyšev ordered Saltykov arrested on April 21, 1848. The writer was sent into exile, not to return until 1855.[19]

Sergej Fedorovič Durov was not as talented as either Dostoevskij or Saltykov, but he had literary aspirations and did manage to build a minor reputation as a poet and translator.[20] A university graduate, he went into banking as a career. As the nephew of the chairman of the Editing Commissions, Durov was able to claim many valuable contacts in St. Petersburg. He joined the Petraševskij circle in early 1847, and in March, 1849, he established his own literary musical discussion group.

One of Durov's most beloved translations, and one which caught the revolutionary *élan* of the *Petraševcy*, was the poem *"Chiaia"*. The author was Henri-Auguste Barbier, a contemporary Frenchman who constantly criticized the regime of Louis-Philippe. The poem was based on the uprising led in 1647 by painter, Salvator Rosa, against the Spaniards near Naples, and it described the attempts of the Carbonari in the 1820s and 1830s to wrest Italian independence from the Neapolitan Bourbons. Barbier's narration of Italy's fight for national integrity struck a responsive chord among the *Petraševcy*, who saw in it

---

[17] S. A. Makašin, *Saltykov-Ščedrin*, I (Moscow, 1951), p. 276.
[18] Makašin, *op. cit.*, I, p. 280.
[19] Makašin, *op. cit.*, I, p. 293.
[20] V. I. Semevskij, "Durov", *Ènciklopedičeskij slovar'*, XIX, p. 167.

parallels to their own struggles under Nicholas.[21] In April, 1849, Durov gained further insight into the nature of revolution when he was arrested with the other *Petraševcy* and later sentenced to death.

Aleksej Nikolaevič Pleščeev was one of the original members of the Petraševskij circle. Another graduate of the University of St. Petersburg, Pleščeev was a poet whose forte was depicting the bureaucratic world of high society. His poem "Forward, Without Fear and Doubt to a Valiant Triumph, Friends" ("Vpered! bez straxa i somnenija na podvig doblestnyj, druz'ja!") was warmly received by his fellow *Petraševcy*.[22] Late in 1848, Pleščeev left Petraševskij and established his own circle, which in turn became the Durov circle. Nevertheless, Pleščeev found himself among those sentenced to die for association with subversives.

The talented poet Apollon Aleksandrovič Grigor'ev (who was no relation to the army officer Nikolaj Grigor'ev, discussed earlier) visited the Fridays during 1845. That same year Grigor'ev wrote a romantic play titled *Two Egos,*[23] the main character of which was named Petuševskij and was described as a "touring Fourierist from Petersburg".[24] Throughout the latter 1840s, many of the themes discussed by the *Petraševcy* appeared in Grigor'ev's poems. Grigor'ev left the circle after a short time, thus avoiding arrest and ruination, and gained considerable fame in the 1860s when he led a movement known as the 'grass-rooters', who attempted to transform the subject matter of literature from abstract humanity into the grassroots spirit of the nation.[25]

Several quite ardent Fourierists could be counted among the *Petraševcy*. Aleksandr Vladimirovič Xanykov was one of them. After graduating from a study of Oriental languages at the University of St. Petersburg, he began attending the *Petraševcy* gatherings in 1845. Xanykov's enthusiasm for Fourierism predated his meeting with Petraševskij and was the cause of his arrest in 1849; in fact, Xanykov was an active Fourierist propagandist. He is recorded as having passed out Fourierist literature at public lectures and having made several

---

[21]   *Poèty-Petraševcy*, ed. V. L. Komarovič (Leningrad, 1957), pp. 359-360.
[22]   *Poèty-Petraševcy*, pp. 269-270.
[23]   Appolon Grigor'ev, "Dva ègoizma", *Izbrannye proizvedenija*, ed. B. Kosteljanec (Leningrad, 1959), pp. 185-268.
[24]   *Poèty-Petraševcy*, p. 319.
[25]   Sergei Pushkarev, *The Emergence of Modern Russia, 1801-1917*, trans. Robert McNeal and Tova Yedlin (New York, 1963), p. 171.

attempts to pay evening calls on families for the purpose of converting them to Fourierism.[26]

The best informed *Petraševec* on the theory of Fourier was Nikolaj Jakovlevič Danilevskij, a Lyceum graduate and a botanist from the University of St. Petersburg. Between 1845 and 1848, he gave a series of lectures on Fourierism at the Petraševskij Fridays.[27] Apparently, the regime found his lectures relatively innocuous, for his arrest in June, 1849, netted him only a three-month jail sentence.

Danilevskij published a work titled *Russia and Europe* (1871) which by 1888 had become a best-seller. In the book, he stated that culturally Russia does not belong to Europe, but that like two separate organisms the two areas would have to remain mutually hostile.[28] He suggested that as an historically Slavic area, Constantinople should be repossessed and be made the capital of the new Russian Empire. Danilevskij's book served as the text for the Slavophiles and Pan-Slavists in the late nineteenth century.

Nikolaj Sergeevič Kaškin, the youngest of the *Petraševcy*, was also an ardent Fourierist. He was born in Kaluga, the son of a Decembrist and a relation of N. A. Serno-Solovevič, one of the founders of the first Populist group, *Land and Liberty (Zemlja i volja)*. His early education in foreign languages was so complete that his father hired a tutor to re-instruct young Kaškin in Russian. He later worked in the Ministry of Foreign Affairs.

Actually, Kaškin is called a *Petraševec* despite the fact that he only attended one meeting at Petraševskij's house. In October, 1848, he established his own circle for the purpose of discussing theoretical Fourierism with other *Petraševcy* who had grown tired of the bickering at Petraševskij's meetings. Kaškin was among those who were sentenced to death in December, 1849, but his sentence was commuted. After a period in exile, Kaškin joined with Serno-Solovevič in efforts to free the serfs in Kaluga province. Kaškin died in 1914 at age eighty-five.

One of Kaškin's closest colleagues among the *Petraševcy* was Dmitrij Dmitrievič Axšarumov. Like Kaškin, and other *Petraševcy*, he was an Oriental literature specialist who worked in the Asiatic section of

[26] V. I. Semevskij, "Propaganda Petraševcev v učebnyx zavedenijax", *Golos minuvšago*, 2 (February 1917), p. 165.
[27] Frank Fadner, *Seventy Years of Pan-Slavism in Russia: Karamzin to Danilevskii, 1800-1870* (Washington, 1961), p. 314.
[28] Fadner, *op. cit.*, p. 320.

the Ministry of Foreign Affairs. Axšarumov was distinguished among those in the Petraševskij circle by the fervor of his belief in spreading propaganda to all levels of society. He was among those sentenced to die after his arrest in 1849.

Another Kaškin associate was Ippolit Matveevič Debu, who agreed with Kaškin and Axšarumov about the importance of Fourierism to a developing Russia. Debu and his brother, also a *Petraševec,* were Roman Catholics of French ancestry.[29] Their grandfather had been an eighteenth-century medical innovator in Russia who, among other things, was the first to innoculate sailors against smallpox.[30] The Debu brothers began visiting Petraševskij's circle in the winter of 1847. Ippolit was arrested in 1849 and exiled.

Aleksandr Ivanovič Evropeus was another close friend of Kaškin, Axšarumov, and Debu who had graduated from the Lyceum and had taken a doctorate in political economy from the University of St. Petersburg. He was arrested in 1849 and exiled but returned to spend much of the rest of his life working for serf reforms.

When Feliks Gustafovič Tol' began visiting Petraševskij in 1846, he brought with him a reputation as an iconoclast and socialist propagandist. As a teacher at the School for Engineers, Tol' had introduced the subjects of socialism and communism into his classes and had drawn the disfavor of the chief of Military Schools.[31] Tol''s specialty was religion and he led the *Petraševcy* discussions of it on several occasions. In philosophy, he stood closer to Petraševskij than did any of the other members of the circle.

Tol' was sentenced to two years' exile in Siberia, at the end of which he chose to remain in Tomsk with Bakunin. In 1859, however, Tol' returned to St. Petersburg and began work on a dictionary similar to Petraševskij's.[32] According to Semevskij, Tol's work included explanations of all the "main socialist terminology, names of scientists, artists, and writers; it included an explanation of all foreign words which had entered the Russian language as well as bibliographical information on various works, magazines and newspapers."[33] Publishing the work him-

---

[29]   There were eight pairs of brothers among the *Petraševcy*: Debu, Axšarumov, Timkovskij, Dostoevskij, Evropeus, Kajdanov, Kuz'min, and Lamanskij.
[30]   V. I. Semevskij, "K. M. i I. M. Debu", *Golos minuvšago,* 2 (February 1916), p. 56.
[31]   Semevskij, "Propaganda Petraševcev", p. 145.
[32]   V. I. Semevskij, "Tol'", *Ènciklopedičeskij slovar',* XXXIII, p. 438.
[33]   Semevskij, *loc. cit.*

self lost Tol' a great deal of money, and he died the year the dictionary appeared.

Pavel Nikolaevič Filippov was a translator of western scientific articles into Russian; he began attending the Petraševskij meetings in 1848. It was Filippov's idea to set up a secret press to print articles of discussion of social issues. His plans came to naught, however, when he was arrested with the other *Petraševcy* and sentenced to death.

Along with Tol' the Lutheran and Debu the Roman Catholic, Ivan-Ferdinand L'vovič Jastžembskij was another non-Orthodox *Petraševec*. He was a Polish Catholic, the only one in the group. Born into the Minsk gentry and a graduate of the University of Kharkov, Jastžembskij taught political economy at the Technological Institute in St. Petersburg. He was quite popular among the *Petraševcy*, a Don Juan, an old bachelor, and a continual arguer. He gave long lectures on political economy at the circle gatherings, lectures in which he supported Fourier's notion that the goal of man is simple harmony. He attacked the government for trying to subordinate "the dignity of the people for its own advantages",[34] and described good government as that "which strives for the development of man's intellect as well as his dignity".[35] As a teacher Jastržembskij tried to instill in his students a sense of indignation at the Russian social system. He posed such delicate questions as "Where does inequality come from?" and "Why is it that some are lucky and others are not?" Given the slimmest opportunity, Jastržembskij attacked the government for draining the people of their self-respect.[36] And he never let his fellow *Petraševcy* forget that although he would gladly sacrifice his own life for the independence of Poland, he would, if necessary, sacrifice Polish sovereignty to the advancement of the socialist ideal.

One of Russia's most famous nineteenth-century economists, Vladimir Alekseevič Miljutin, was an early participant in the Petraševskij circle. A political economist and professor at the University of St. Petersburg, Vladimir Miljutin was the brother of a future Minister of War, Dmitrij; the brother of Nikolaj Miljutin, who helped draw up regulations for the abolition of serfdom in 1861; and the nephew of P. D. Kiselev, chief of the Fifth Section. Miljutin left the circle with Saltykov in 1847, thus avoiding arrest.[37]

---

[34] V. A. Desnitskij (ed.), *Delo Petraševcev*, III (Moscow, 1951), p. 418.
[35] Desnickij, *op. cit.*, III, p. 419.
[36] Semevskij, "Propaganda Petraševcev", p. 139.
[37] Lekjina, *Petraševcy*, p. 143.

The oldest *Petraševec* was Aleksandr Pantalejmonovič Balasoglo, who was ten years older than the average age of the *Petraševcy*. Balasoglo had no formal education, but had taught himself several Oriental languages and was an expert on Russo-Asian history and politics. He worked in both the Ministry of Education and in the Ministry of Foreign Affairs. As a member of the newly-founded Russian Geographical Society, Balasoglo helped organize an 1846 expedition to Siberia and the Pacific and aided Admiral G. I. Nevel'skoj in finding a passage from the mouth of the Amur to the Pacific Ocean. The following year he made an historical survey of Moscow's colonization of Siberia.[38]

Balasoglo was one of Petraševskij's first visitors in 1845, and a great admirer of the young reformer's ideas. Balasoglo was especially interested in increasing the number of bookstores and libraries in Russia. He was convinced that only through the spread of the *Petraševcy's* socialist ideas could reform come to Russia. When the other *Petraševcy* were arrested, Balasoglo was fortunate enough to suffer only a short period of surveillance.

Vasilij Andreevič Golovinskij was, with Petraševskij himself, one of the few *Petraševcy* with legal training. Actually, Golovinskij only attended two meetings in Petraševskij's house; he was a regular member of the Durov circle. He was well-received at Petraševskij's meeting, however, when he attended once in April, 1849, to deliver a resounding speech on the need for freeing the serfs.[39] After his arrest, Golovinskij was exiled to Siberia for eight years .

After his return to Russia, Golovinskij participated in preparations for the emancipation of the serfs in Simbirsk province. But in 1858, he was charged by the landowners with showing favoritism to the peasants and was forced to flee to Tver', where he became a close friend of Saltykov.

Aleksandr Petrovič Beklemišev was chief of the Ministry of Internal Affairs office in Revel' when he visited Petraševskij's circle in 1849. In fact, Beklemišev was the employer of K. I. Timkovskij, the *Petraševec* who attempted to establish Fourierist discussion groups in Revel'. Like Golovinskij, he impressed the *Petraševcy* with his ringing speeches denouncing serfdom and advocating the organization of the peasants into Fourierist communes. Beklemišev was not arrested but was put under surveillance for a short time. In 1851, he was appointed Vice-Governor of Kurland, and from 1858 to 1868 he served as governor of Mogilev,

[38] Lejkina, *op. cit.*, p. 113.
[39] V. I. Semevskij, "Golovinskij", *Ènciklopedičeskij slovar'*, XV, p. 333.

thus becoming the only *Petraševec* to attain high position in the Russian government.

These men were, of course, but a few of the hundreds touched by Petraševskij's influence. These, however, were the most notable in terms of their participation in the circle's meetings and discussions and their fervor in arguing and working for a new Russia under socialism.

V

MECHANICS OF COMMUNICATION:
THE DISCUSSION GROUPS

In 1845, following the death of his father, Petraševskij moved from the family home into a house of his own, located near the heart of St. Petersburg on Pokrovskaja Square (now called Turgenev Square). Here, in the fall of that year, he began to gather about him the circle of friends, acquaintances, and, later, complete strangers whose influence would grow over the next four years to proportions which roused the fear and anger of the Tsar.

Originally, only five or six young men joined the twenty-four year-old Petraševskij for informal Friday evening discussions of the socialist theories of Fourier. As others joined the circle, they agreed among themselves that the meetings were excellent means for furthering their educations – and little more. For the first two years, the *Petraševcy* studied and discussed socialism on a rather abstract plane. They heeded Petraševskij's advice that "before we begin to act we must study" [1] and collected books; N. A. Mombelli, for one, had accumulated 135 Russian books and 454 foreign books by the time of his arrest in 1849.

Petraševskij apparently never refused anyone admittance to the Friday evening gatherings. On a given Friday, the circle might include students, army officers, low-ranking bureaucrats, sons of important government figures, secondary school teachers, university professors, and people known in literary and musical circles. No one, however, ever noted having seen foreigners, women, or clergymen at the 'Fridays'.

The *Petraševcy* were young spirits, most of them in their early twenties, well-bred and serious. They saw the Fridays as enriching experiences, by far preferable to the card games and liberal chatter of the usual congregations of St. Petersburg's young people. They gathered to exchange frank views through conversation, the reading of articles and debate. They were apparently reassured by Petraševskij's belief that his

[1] V. R. Lejkina-Svirskaja, *Petraševcy* (Moscow, 1965), p. 30.

house was somehow a sanctuary from the prying police, and each member felt free to pour out his heart when more sober reflection might have kept him quiet. One observer, the liberal economist K. S. Veselovskij, noted later that much of what was said in the heat of argument at Petraševskij's house might have been left unsaid under other circumstances.[2]

Although each individual was allowed to voice serious opinions on that 'science' with which he was most familiar, the predominant topic for discussion was socialism, with Fourierism often at the focus of attention. There was seldom any general agreement on any matter, but nearly everyone enjoyed the free give-and-take of the discussions.

In recalling the Friday meetings, Balasoglo used the noun 'society' (*obščestvo*).[3] However, there were no initiations or secret rites among the *Petraševcy*. There were no particular rules governing what the participants could or could not do. Actually, those attending Petraševskij's discussions were bound only by mutual interests in socialism and social reform and by their common youth. Balasoglo was probably more nearly correct when he described the circle as a "single family, only not a family by blood relationship, but simply a spiritual and secular family, a family bound together by living together and science".[4]

Until late in 1848, when the attendance rose sharply to a high of seventy on one evening, only some seven to ten people appeared regularly at Petraševskij's house for conversation. On such occasions as someone's name day or birthday, as many as fifty would attend. For the last six months of the group's existence, weekly attendance averaged between twenty and forty people.[5]

Petraševskij was always eager to show a book or an idea from the West to his visitors. He seemed easily able to interest group members in completely new subjects. He directed the discussions as much as possible toward the socialist thinkers, especially those who advocated a 'perfect' utopian state and who believed in the principle of association in some form. The French utopians Etienne Cabet and Pierre Leroux were read and discussed by the *Petraševcy*, who found fascinating the phalanstery-like communal organizations established by each of them.

Pavel Konstantinovič Mart'janov visited a Petraševskij Friday meet-

---

[2] K. S. Veselovskij, "Vospominanija o nekotoryx licejskix tovariščax", *Russkaja starina*, 9 (September 1900), p. 452.
[3] V. I. Semevskij, *Sobranie sočinenij: M. V. Butaševič-Petraševskij i Petraševcy*, ed. V. V. Vodovozov, II (Moscow, 1922), p. 105.
[4] Semevskij, *loc. cit.*
[5] Semevskij, *op. cit.*, p. 106.

ing in 1848. He later recalled that there were ten to fifteen guests, including a sprinkling of military men. New guests were welcomed cordially, Mart'janov noted, and a spirit of general conviviality reigned. A large samovar stood in the hall and nearby were wine and *zakuski*. Mart'janov's recollections make no mention of any whiff of subversiveness at the gathering.

Others were not so impressed with the innocence of the *Petraševcy*, however. The famous musician, Anton Grigor'evič Rubinštejn, visited Petraševskij's house in 1849, when he was eighteen years old. He was thoroughly amazed and shocked by the reading of a treatise on socialism:

I didn't expect to meet with something like this in Russia. I understood that such readings and thoughts are expressed abroad where the social conditions are so different from ours. But we didn't have any place in Russia for such thinking! [6]

The young Rubinštejn openly argued with Petraševskij, a forwardness which may have later saved him from arrest, since at least one government agent was probably there that evening. Later that week, Petraševskij visited Rubinštejn, bought him several foreign liberal books, and discussed social reform with him at great length; however, there is no record whether or not Petraševskij made a Fourierist convert out of the young musician.

The outbreak of the February Revolution of 1848 in France made a deep impression on the *Petraševcy*. In March of that year, a sense of discipline was felt among them for the first time. In their earlier criticism of the government, they had clung to the notion that if the Tsar knew what was going on in the country, he would initiate reforms. Nicholas' close advisors, the *Petraševcy* felt, were keeping all pertinent information from him. With the political upheavals of France as their inspiration, the circle members began to be more openly critical of the Emperor himself. Petraševskij began encouraging propaganda efforts among the group, citing the failure of the Decembrists to share their revolution with all social levels. The question of reform in general and the peasant problem in particular became the chief topics of discussion.

One of the results of this new discipline and direction among the *Petraševcy* was the aroused interest of the police. On March 11, 1849, a new visitor presented himself at Petraševskij's door. He was Petr Dmi-

---

[6] P. E. Ščegolev (ed.), *Petraševcy*, III (Moscow, 1928), p. 111.

trievič Antonelli, an agent of General Liprandi in the Ministry of the Interior. Liprandi had hand-picked young Antonelli to infiltrate the Fridays, and the general's plan worked beautifully. Of the ten *Petraševcy* in attendance that evening, Feliks Tol' argued most violently against Antonelli's admittance; Tol' suspected what later proved to be true about Antonelli's police connections. But Petraševskij himself befriended the uninvited newcomer and Antonelli was allowed to stay. From that day until April 23, when the *Petraševcy* were arrested, Antonelli was present at every meeting, sometimes brazenly taking notes which he would later transcribe into full reports for General Liprandi.

Not all the *Petraševcy* were happy with the type and means of discussion at the gatherings. Certain modifications were made in the format of the meetings: Petraševskij surrendered leadership to a system whereby a different President served every week, although he reserved the privilege of telling the President when to ring the bell that ended the discussion of one topic and signaled the opening of a new one.[7] At Pavel Kuz'min's suggestion, each meeting was split into two periods, the first devoted to Russian social questions, the second – following dinner – devoted to socialist theory in general. It was also decided that only specialists would talk on assigned topics. If Petraševskij did not assign one a topic, then he could not make a speech.

Still there were those who felt their views were not being aired or who felt Petraševskij was too lax in his selection of the guests. So toward the end of 1848, Pleščeev, Spešnev, and Dostoevskij began meeting at Pleščeev's house. From this group evolved the Durov circle, led by Durov, Dostoevskij, and Pal'm. On March 1, 1849, these three, bored with political discussions in general and Petraševskij's views in particular, met for the first time to discuss art and music. Their circle grew to include Spešnev, N. P. Grigor'ev, Pavel Filippov and others.

The members of the Durov circle – the *Durovcy* – paid dues of three rubles a month, which Durov used to buy food and drink and to rent a piano. One person was appointed to supervise the discussions, but the free-wheeling *Durovcy* usually paid him little heed. Despite their original organization as a literary circle, the *Durovcy* soon outstripped the *Petraševcy* in their revolutionary fervor. They were the first to discuss ways of spreading propaganda among the army. Grigor'ev wrote a short description of a "Conversation between Soldiers" on the unpleasantness of army life.[8] When he read it aloud before the *Durovcy*, however, the

[7] V. A. Desnitskij (ed.), *Delo Petraševcev*, III (Moscow, 1951), p. 116.

[8] V. E. Evgrafov (ed.), *Filosofskie i obščestvenno-političeskie proizvedenija Petra-*

response was meager and Mixail Dostoevskij, who often played the calming influence among the *Durovcy*, urged Grigor'ev to destroy the piece. Despite the fact that the army would have been a fertile field for agitation, it is probable that military men such as L'vov and Pal'm rejected the proposal.

A small group of the *Durovcy* decided to set up a secret printing press in the home of Spešnev's friend Nikolaj Aleksandrovič Mordvinov. Young Mordvinov had close connections within the regime, an advantage which later saved him from arrest and kept the police from finding the press even though they knew of its existence.[9] The *Durovcy* plan to print and distribute the speeches read at their meetings was never carried out.

In October of 1848, another group of dissidents left the Petraševskij circle because talk of actual revolution was beginning. These men – including Nicholaj Kaškin, Dmitrij Axšarumov, the Debu brothers, the Evropeus brothers, and others – formed what came to be known as the Kaškin circle, which stated as its aim "the study of the unique system of Fourier as the truth for the whole world, to which goal all humanity is constantly striving".[10] The *Kaškincy* were "purist" Fourierists; Fourier held such strong views against revolution, for instance, that the subject was forbidden at the *Kaškincy* meetings. Instead, they discussed:

only what was found in the works of Fourier, about his views on the capability of man, about the means of finding the kind of work which each person was best fitted, and of making labor a pleasant task instead of a burden, about the meaning of all humanity and the significance of our planet in the solar system.[11]

The Kaškin circle took the initiative in giving a dinner on the anniversary of Fourier's birthday, April 7, 1849. The event took place in the home of A. I. Evropeus, but Kaškin issued the invitations. Eleven guests arrived, including Petraševskij, who was quite miffed at having been upstaged by Kaškin's Fourierist loyalty. The party was a thorough success. Kaškin had ordered a huge portrait of Fourier shipped from Paris and it hung like an icon behind the head of the table. Throughout the evening toasts and speeches were dedicated to Fourier. Kaškin read Pierre de Berranger's poem "Fools", which was in honor of Fourier.

ševcev (Moscow, 1953), pp. 645-649.
[9] V. R. Lejkina, *Petraševcy* (Moscow, 1924), p. 32.
[10] Desnitskij, *op. cit.*, III, p. 175.
[11] Desnitskij, *op. cit.*, III, p. 118.

Ippolit Debu made a speech insisting that all of Fourier's work be translated into Russian. Accordingly, within the next few days, those who were guests at the dinner were assigned one hundred pages of the *Théorie de l'unité universelle*. The translations were never finished, for the *Petraševcy* were arrested only two weeks later.

One of the most significant contributions which Petraševskij himself made to the *Petraševcy*, including those who visited other circles, was his creation of a collective library for the members' use. In 1846, he established a program to which depositors contributed from fifteen to thirty rubles a year. Petraševskij assumed the responsibility of ordering books from lists of Western editions sold by Russian booksellers. He also catalogued the circle's purchases in the library, which was located in his house. The *Petraševcy* had access to these books and to Petraševskij's personal library as well, and thereby developed many common political viewpoints.

The *Kaškincy* also had a library, a collection begun in 1848. Upon payment of a ten ruble fee, any *Kaškinec* or *Petraševec* could borrow from the library, but his choice would be limited to works by Fourier and Considérant.

Although there was a great amount of western European socio-political literature in Russia during the late 1840s, the Tsarist government had relatively little success in controlling it. According to one account, between 1832 and 1849 more than nine million foreign books entered Russia.[12] Of the several hundred thousand that entered every year, the regime's censor was able to inspect only about 21,000 books. Of those censored, approximately 2,600 were forbidden "for the public"; another 2,600 were passed after objectionable passages were removed. But once a book was smuggled into Russia, it circulated freely; many foreign books on the censor's restricted list were readily available. The bookseller Iosif Karlovič Luri, one of many who traded in forbidden books, served as supplier to the *Petraševcy* library. Nearly three thousand forbidden books were found in Luri's store in April, 1849.[13]

Books may well have been one of the strongest inducements for young Russians to visit Petraševskij's Fridays. They certainly were a highly effective means of spreading socialist ideas among the *Petraševcy*; some books were passed from member to member, interesting portions underlined and marginal notes made with which the members could then note

---

[12] Lejkina-Svirskaja, *op. cit.*, p. 33.
[13] Lejkina-Svirskaja, *op. cit.*, p. 34.

their agreement or disagreement. But the discussion meetings at Petraševskij's house – representing as they did open forums for free discussion of ideas which were burning in the hearts of many young Russians
and engendering like groups across St. Petersburg – were doubtless the
principal deep well from which poured the flow of socialist reform thinking of the 1840s.

VI

SOCIAL AND POLITICAL THOUGHT OF THE *PETRAŠEVCY*

In the course of their Friday discussions, most of the *Petraševcy* became familiar with many of the trends in socialist thinking which were emanating from western Europe in the 1840s. But of the various ideologies with which the group came into contact – Saint-Simonism, Owenism, the ideas of Proudhon, Raspail, Vidal, Villegardelle, and Louis Blanc – by far the most influential was Fourierism. For along with offering answers to the political and social questions which the *Petraševcy* were raising among themselves, Fourierism also provided a whole concept of personal and social life. The words of Fourier soundly criticized capitalism while devising a model for social re-organization; they suggested the key to harmony among men and the means for achieving an egalitarian economic lift-off in Russia.

The leading Fourierist theoretician among the *Petraševcy* was Nikolaj Jakovlevič Danilevskij. Although he gave a series of lectures titled "The Teaching of Fourier" ("Učenie Fur'e") at Petraševskij's house during the first four months of 1848, little of what he said was recorded. What is known of Danilevskij's critique of Fourierism was set down by him in his written testimony before the Investigative Commission in mid-1849.[1]

An understanding of Danilevskij's interpretation of Fourierism is essential to an understanding of the strength of Fourier's influence upon the *Petraševcy*. Danilevskij, much more detailed in his discussion of Fourierism than Petraševskij, has given a clear account of those elements of the Fourierist system which seemed to make it particularly appealing to the young Russian reformers.

All 'beings' (*suščestva*), both animate and inanimate, Danilevskij states, are subject to certain unchanging laws.[2] By these laws, which

---

[1] V. R. Lejkina, *Petraševcy* (Moscow, 1924), pp. 87-111. Also found in P. E. Ščegolev (ed.), *Petraševcy*, II (Moscow, 1927), pp. 118-149.

[2] It is of interest to note that Danilevskij had no more use for Fourier's views on inanimate objects in the cosmogony than did Petraševskij. He was interested only in Fourierist teachings which would improve the human lot.

Danilevskij implies are based on Newton's theories, the being with consciousness will seek 'happiness' as the goal of its development; this search for happiness finds the being (man, the only being with consciousness) striving toward a harmonious condition for itself and for those beings around it. The process, however, is a slow one. The being endures first a period of chaos during which he is distracted by secondary influences. Out of this chaos the individual must discover which scientific means to selfknowledge (*samo-znanie*), and thereby to true harmony, is best for him.

Danilevskij categorically reduces to two the number of pathways to harmony: man must pursue either *a priori* or *a posteriori* methods. "*A priori* methods give false results", he says. "They do not bring happiness."[3] The difficulty with such methods is their assumption of equality, which Danilevskij questions as a fundamental law. "Man thirsts not for equality or freedom but happiness."[4] *A posteriori* methods, on the other hand, demand that the individual experience both success and failure, thus coming into selfknowledge and into a state of harmony with his environment.

Danilevskij wrote at some length on the vicissitudes of the twelve passions *(strasti)*, as enunciated by Fourier and by Petraševskij.[5] Universal satisfaction of these passions demands first a higher standard of living, which Fourier suggests can be achieved by increasing production. Overruling the Malthusian theory that population increases will outstrip production increases, Danilevskij offers three conditions which determine the forces of production in society: 1) the raw materials which are still in a state of nature, 2) the ability of the scientific community to make the best use of these materials for the betterment of mankind, and 3) the economic organization of the society, which determines how successfully the scientists will be able to use the economic potential. In view of these factors, Danilevskij says, it is quite possible to raise the standard of living by increasing production.

In revealing the key to the economic organization of society, Danilevskij cites a central Fourierist doctrine: the principle of association. Through the principle of association, the twelve passions can be satisfied and man brought into a state of harmony. It is through the principle of association, Danilevskij states, that the improbable goal of making labor attractive to the worker can be reached.

3   Lejkina, *op. cit.*, p. 88.
4   Lejkina, *loc. cit.*
5   See "Petraševskij and Fourierism", p. 26.

From the principle of association, Danilevskij derives his 'law of the series' *(seriarnyj zakon)*, which he bases on the assumption that it is as wrong to make a man a slave to his job as it is to leave him idle. He lists seven reasons why labor is unpleasant: the long duration of labor; the monotony, the solitariness, the complexity, the inefficiency and the lack of intrigue which are characteristic of labor; and the constraints placed upon the laborer by the task itself. By utilizing the law of the series, Danilevskij suggests, and by varying the duration of each of the twelve passions, a new work scheme could provide passion gratification for the individual and make labor more attractive.

Danilevskij chose hay mowing as a typical task with which to illustrate the law of the series work scheme, typical because as an aspect of agricultural production it was the sort of endeavor in which the majority of Russians were employed. According to Danilevskij's plan, many laborers would be engaged in the multitude of separate tasks involved in hay mowing, but no one would feel alone or alienated because each person would feel he was part of a giant team working toward a common goal. Boredom would be alleviated by having all the workers taking turns in the various tasks: each man would cut the grass for awhile, then bind the sheaves, then switch to loading bales on wagons, and so on. Each worker aids his fellow; there is no room for egoists in Danilevskij's model hay field.

Competition is introduced between groups of hay cutters, men competing with men and women competing with women. At a great dinner held at the end of haying season, awards are presented to the competition winners in much the same way that awards were given to the strongest and most skillful ancient Greek warriors. The haying champions of one phalanx would have the honor of participating in the haying at neighboring phalanxes.

Danilevskij's vision of cooperative hay mowing extended beyond national borders. His writing foresees a time when mighty armies of laborers could be assembled from all the world's countries for concentration in such areas as the Llanos and the Pampas of South America, where great quantities of hay must be cut and housed annually. International companies of actors and actresses, he continues, could be sent along to provide lavish entertainment for the workers. Regardless of the scale of the haying operation, however, no one laborer will have the opportunity to get individually ambitious because he will change from job to job as many as forty times. When he is not working at a particular task, he can occupy his time by cheering on those who are engaged in some especially distasteful job.

Such a work scheme would be feasible, Danilevskij writes, if the peasants and agricultural workers were organized into an association at the phalanx level. Retaining his own private property, each individual enters the association by making a financial contribution *(dolja)* for which he receives a share *(akcija)*. His share of the association is much like a share of common stock: its value rises and falls with the rising and falling of the price of "that immoveable property for which it is the moveable substitute *(dvižimyj predstavitel')*".[6] The owner may sell or give away or do whatever he wishes with his share. At the end of the year, the entire income of the phalanx is divided among the member-shareholders. Danilevskij suggested division of the proceeds into twelfths, with four-twelfths set aside for capital, five-twelfths set aside for labor, and three-twelfths set aside for talent (or qualities of leadership). He allowed, however, for changes in these proportions as local conditions demanded.

The allocation of the portion set aside for capital is simply done: each member is paid according to the size of his share. But Danilevskij becomes a bit vague when he treats the division of the labor and talent portions of the association's income. Following Fourier, Danilevskij divides labor into the categories of necessary labor without which the phalanx could not survive, useful labor and pleasant labor. Those performing the necessary labor receive the largest portion, those performing the pleasant labor receive the smallest. The enthusiasm which one displays for his work is a criterion for capital distribution.

Only the leaders of the worker groups are eligible for portions of the talent allocation. The administration of the phalanx makes a preliminary estimate *(smeta)* of these leaders' qualifications. Those receiving the highest marks then stand a common vote *(obščaja ballotirovka),* which in Danilevskij's view was the most accurate and just way of selecting the recipients of the talent shares of the income.

The inheritance of private property, including shares in the association, must be maintained, Danilevskij felt, because to deny it would be an infringement upon the passion of parenthood. He suggested, however, that inheritances should be equally divided among heirs to avoid jealousy; inheritance, he pointed out, was not based on one's labor or talent contribution to the community.

⁶   Lejkina, *op. cit.*, p. 104.

While not defending Fourier's position on the family, incidentally, Danilevskij did deny that the phalanstery fostered sexual immorality. He felt that relations between the sexes should be freer, but that Fourier's ideas of mixing the sexes could not be realized for at least 300 years.

In his final analysis of the Fourierist system, Danilevskij outlined what he believed to be the best economic organization of society. If labor could be made attractive, then Malthus' prophecy of the fatal overpopulation of the world would be proved wrong. Through the machinations of the association and with an increase in the production of goods, the poor would be made richer and the rich would lose some of their wealth. Further, "the distribution of all the activities of man through the group and series, having destroyed the struggle of interests and the collision of the passions, will destroy the very source and root of dissensions, vices and crimes."[7] Moreover, Danilevskij believed that the Fourierist system could be instituted without upsetting the foundations upon which governmental and personal life were based. The system would maintain Russian social tradition, he said, because it held that "the idea of equality is not only an impossible dream but is harmful and incompatible with human nature and with the claims of the 'law of the series'; the 'law of the series' demands inequality in all relations."[8]

Danilevskij's rendition of the Fourierist concept of association impressed the Petraševcy at large, but most particularly Vladimir Alekseevič Miljutin. Miljutin, whose numerous writings on the agricultural problems of western Europe had earned him the respect of his fellow *Petraševcy*, stated that "the two fundamental tendencies of modern agricultural economy were on the one hand the transference of land to the peasants and, on the other, the increasingly obvious advantage to be derived from large farms."[9] These seemingly contradictory tendencies could best be resolved, Miljutin thought, through association. To him, association meant the establishment of peasant cooperatives – resembling Fourier's phalanstery system – all over Russia. The peasant farms, as Miljutin conceived them, were comparable to the large state farms later established as experimental farms in the Soviet Union.

Fedor Nikolaevič L'vov pinpointed a principal weakness in the con-

[7] Lejkina, *op. cit.*, p. 108.
[8] Lejkina, *op. cit.*, p. 109.
[9] V. A. Miljutin, *Izbrannye proizvedenija*, ed. I. G. Bljumin (Moscow, 1946), p. 350, as quoted in Franco Venturi, *Roots of Revolution*, trans. Francis Haskel (New York, 1960), p. 79.

cept of association as articulated by Danilevskij. The hay mowing example would not apply to industrial production because, as L'vov
pointed out, factories employed highly specialized labor. While the
'law of the series' called for continual changes of occupation to prevent
boredom in the workers, a factory specialist knew only one operation.
Furthermore, modern industrial efficiency depends upon highly skilled
laborers; Danilevskij's plan offered no suggestions for adapting his
serial organization of agricultural workers to the needs of an industrial-
ized society. This basic weakness of Fourierism is, perhaps, one reason
why it failed to develop in revolutionary Russia.

By 1848, Danilevskij was ready to follow Petraševskij's lead and try
his hand at building a phalanstery. As he outlined his plan to the Petraševcy, four or five million rubles and three or four thousand *desjatiny*
of land could easily be appropriated for the project. He called for 1,500
to 2,000 people of both sexes, of all ages, of various education who
showed ability in their studies to come together in his association.[10]
But nothing ever came of his idea, and Danilevskij's interest in Fourierism seems to have waned. In May, 1848, he delivered his last Friday
evening lecture on Fourier and left the Petraševskij circle to continue
his studies in botany.

Konstantin Ivanovič Timkovskij proposed a slightly more involved
plan than Danilevskij's. From Petraševskij's experience in phalanstery
construction, Timkovskij concluded that the masses were too ignorant
to appreciate the value of the concept. He therefore proposed a sweep-
ing propaganda campaign aimed at the higher, more intellectual circles
of society. After the three years necessary for the campaign, Timkovskij
said, he would then request from the government permission to build a
phalanstery. If permission were granted, he would appeal for governmental funds to construct the buildings. If the government refused to
risk the money, those who were convinced of the worthiness of the
cause should form a company of shareholders which would finance the
construction. Timkovskij's proposal found no support whatsoever; not
a man of the *Petraševcy* believed that the government would ever give
the initial permission.[11]

In his tract "From the Correspondence of Two Landowners" ("Iz
perepiski dvux pomeščikov"), delivered before the Petraševcy, Aleksandr Petrovič Beklemišev stressed his support for the proposition of

[10]   V. I. Semevskij, *Sobranie sočinenij: M. V. Butaševič-Petraševskij i Petraševcy,*
ed. V. V. Vodovozov, II (Moscow, 1922), p. 119.
[11]   Semevskij, *Petraševskij i Petraševcy,* p. 125.

making labor more attractive to the peasants on gentry estates. The serial organization of agricultural labor, he felt, would increase production. Beklemišev went on to propose that the landowners also participate in the division of labor.

On the question of allotting land to the peasants who had tilled it, Beklemišev cautioned against wholesale division of the large estates before legal matters such as the rightful ownership of the estate were settled. Moreover, he declared that such a land reform program might do more harm than good. Work would be increased and livestock values decreased if the large farms were broken up. A large association farm could operate more efficiently than a number of smaller farms: five or six cooks could feed many people from one large kitchen, thus freeing others for work in the fields. Groups of ten women each could alternate doing laundry for an entire large farm more efficiently than could each woman do laundry for her own family. The rotation of chores would make these domestic tasks more attractive, too. But large farms and large numbers of people cooperating in their operation were indispensable, Beklemišev stated, for the most effective application of the principle of association.[12]

Enthusiasm among the *Petraševcy* for Fourierist ideals of economic organization of labor and communality was not unanimous, however; Dostoevskij felt that the whole system was absurd, "a peaceful system which bewitched the soul by its elegance".[13] Actually, Dostoevskij saw many of the virtues of Fourierism. He acknowledged that Fourierism did not attempt to enforce discipleship, but instilled love for humanity instead. He admitted that it should be thought of as an economic system rather than a political system. It could not be the catalyst for revolution; Dostoevskij recalled that in February, 1848, Fourierists "did not come out on the streets of Paris but remained working on their journal where they had already spent twenty years in dreaming about the future beauty of the phalanstery".[14]

Dostoevskij's criticism of Fourierism revolved around two central points. In the first place, he felt, Fourierism was harmful simply because it was a system. Secondly, he declared that because it was utopian in character it could never be realistically developed. Dostoevskij was more amused than frightened by Fourierism when he wrote:

[12]   V. I. Semevskij, "Petraševcy A. P. Beklemišev i K. I. Timkovskij", *Vestnik Evropy*, 10 (November 1916), p. 65.
[13]   N. F. Bel'čikov, *Dostoevskij v processe Petraševcev* (Moscow, 1936), p. 91.
[14]   Bel'čikov, *op. cit.*, p. 92.

There is no social system which is more unpopular, more hissed at, than the system of Fourier in the West. It died a long time ago and the leaders did not notice that they were living and nothing more. In the West, in France at this minute, every system, every theory is harmful for society. A hungry proletariat in despair seizes at every means to make itself a flag. There hunger runs out on the street. But Fourierism is forgotten out of contempt for it. What touches us in Russia, in St. Petersburg, is that one only has to go twenty feet out in the street in order to convince oneself that Fourierism on our soil can only exist in the pages of a book or in the soft, mild soul of a dreamer, in no other way than in the form of an ideal or a similar poem ... But Fourierism along with other western systems is so uncomfortable for our soil, so contrary to our way of life, so not in the character of our nation.[15]

In linking the proletariat with the development of Fourierism, Dostoevskij was unique among the *Petraševcy,* who believed that Fourierist concepts should be based on agrarian communes. Since Russia had not developed a proletariat like that of the West, he said, "Fourierism would be laughingly funny."[16]

The relationship between Dostoevskij and Petraševskij was always stormy, and Dostoevskij contributed to the mutual ill will by suggesting that Petraševskij had no more than a parlor appreciation of Fourierism. But whatever his feelings toward Petraševskij, Dostoevskij was no more opposed to Fourierism than he was to the other Socialist systems. In fact, he enjoyed discussing Fourierist theories and often expressed his approval of the principle of association.

Saltykov and Muljutin joined Dostoevskij in criticizing Fourierism's weaknesses. Saltykov complained that Fourier's doctrines insisted too strenuously on things "which in the future might or might not happen".[17] His colleagues should not take the system too seriously, he cautioned, for "the attractiveness of labor becomes lost in too much detail".[18] Despite his feeling that without utopias life would be unbearable, Saltykov scored the utopians for their lack of realism. In his novel *Contradictions (Protivorečie),* the principle character Nagibin says, "I am no utopian because the utopia is withdrawn from the historical development of reality."[19]

Miljutin led the battle against the abstractness of the utopians' ideal-

---

[15]   Bel'čikov, *loc. cit.*
[16]   Bel'čikov, *loc. cit.*
[17]   V. I. Semevskij, *Krepostnoe pravo i krest'janskaja reforma v proizvedenijax Mixaila Evgrafoviča Saltykova* (St. Petersburg, 1906), p. 96.
[18]   Semevskij, *Krepostnoe pravo,* p. 97.
[19]   S. A. Makašin, *Saltykov-Ščedrin,* I (Moscow, 1951), p. 243.

ism; theory and practice in their thinking were too far apart to suit him. Utopian theory, he said, had to be brought into a closer relationship with life. Neither he nor Saltykov considered any one utopia better suited for Russia than any other; neither believed in any particular socialist system. For this reason, both men, along with Valerian Nikolaevič Majkov, stopped visiting the Fridays in 1847.

Ippolit Matveevič Debu, on the other hand, saw in Fourierism a system which "would build a society where all our passions are brought to a harmonious development and directed to the single goal of finding full satisfaction for our passions".[20] Debu was particularly delighted with Fourier's teachings of free love and his attack on matrimony, which he described as an act of prostitution that encouraged promiscuity and further prostitution outside of wedlock. This condition "led to a moral and economic lowering of the standards of society".[21] Furthermore, Fourier had written, "prostitution makes use of free love for the decomposition and corruption of people, but in a socialist society free love would only stimulate them to useful labor."[22]

Debu carried on Fourier's attacks on marriage, stating that fathers became slaves to their children. So many vices were hidden under the guise of marriage, he went on, because people were afraid to speak of them openly. Because of marriage, man could never express his true feelings, speaking instead just the opposite from what he felt. Society was responsible for this stifling of the passions, Debu argued, because society condoned marriage.

The most vexing problem for the *Petraševcy* was the adoption of the best means for introducing into Russia the Fourierist system as expatiated by Danilevskij and Petraševskij. Ippolit Debu favored introducing Fourier's law of the series in agriculture and in factories and mills. Stressing "the anti-revolutionary character of Fourierist propaganda in France",[23] Debu and Aleksandr Evropeus suggested hopefully that the government might help to introduce the system into the country. But Debu and the other members of the Kaškin circle (Konstantin Debu, Aleksandr and Pavel Evropeus, Nikolaj Kaškin, Dmitrij Axšarumov, and Aleksandr Xanykov) seldom discussed seriously the means of realizing Fourierism in Russia. They calculated that a phalanstery

[20] V. E. Evgrafov (ed.), *Filosofskie i obščestvenno-političeskie proizvedenija Petraševcev* (Moscow, 1953), p. 108.
[21] Hubert Bourgin, *Fourier: Contribution à l'étude du socialisme français* (Paris, 1905), p. 214.
[22] Bourgin, *op. cit.*, p. 359.
[23] V. A. Desnitskij (ed.), *Delo Petraševcev*, III (Moscow, 1941), p. 177.

of 2,000 people could be built for no less than twenty million rubles, a sum that could not be raised even in ten years.[24] So for the present, Fourierism could only be studied.

The Kaškin circle members were specifically opposed to any attempt to force Fourierism upon Russia. They took as their example the French Fourierists under the leadership of Victor Considérant, who after Fourier's death in 1837 set up schools rather than political parties and showed no interest in mounting a revolt.[25] Kaškin and his friends echoed the French Fourierists' hope that government would take the initiative in establishing the law of the series and thus transform all of society peacefully. They felt that by not antagonizing the regime, they increased the possibility of the introduction of Fourierism; in this respect they were following the policy of Petraševskij, who recommended that his fellow reformers remain meek before the government. There is no record of the Kaškin circle ever having approached the Tsar on the matter of Fourierism.

Aleksandr Xanykov admitted that "Fourierism could not be accepted immediately . . . because of the great amount of ignorance in the present day organization of society."[26] But he also declared:

We are not afraid of this struggle . . . because we have supporters in all ends of the earth who will battle in the name of this law. The overthrow is near; it will not occur through faith and prayer as Christianity teaches but because of pure science we will acquire courage which will give us the endurance to win out in the end.[27]

As we have already noted, Nikolaj Alexandrovič Spešnev was conspicuous among the *Petraševcy* as the group's most frenetic revolutionary, his vehemence and apparent commitment far surpassing Xanykov's. His account "Affair" ("Delo") has been lost, so there is no record of his response to Danilevskij's interpretation of the economic organization of labor. But there is record of his proposal of the formation of a secret revolutionary society in Russia, and there is ample evidence of his having been influenced in this by the theories of the French communist, Theodore Dezamy (1803-1850) and those of the German communist, Wilhelm Christian Weitling. Since the influence of the latter was

---

[24]   V. I. Semevskij, "Kružok Kaškina", *Golos minuvšago*, 4 (April 1916), p. 175.
[25]   Desnitskij, *op. cit.*, III, p. 19.
[26]   Desnitskij, *loc. cit.*
[27]   Desnitskij, *op. cit.*, III, pp. 21-22.

apparently the stronger, some of Weitling's political thinking should be examined.

Weitling was a pre-Marxian communist who founded his principles in the early Christian communal tradition of definite moral precepts and absolute equality. His declared mission was the protection of the existing society from all threats, including society's own past; revolution, he believed, was the means of breaking the death-grip of that past. Society could not be purified through pacificism.

He saw himself as the second Messiah and his teaching called upon men to practice love; he called for a reforming return to primitive Christianity, helping to found what amounted to a modern sect of Anabaptists. Under the Ten Commandments as the supreme law, Weitling's envisioned society would abolish private property and right of inheritance. Governments would be elected democratically.

His book *Humanity As It Is and As It Should Be (Die Menscheit wie sie ist und wie sie sein sollte)*, published in 1839, described Weitling's attempts to integrate the workers' movement.[28] In 1836 Weitling had joined the League of the Just *(Bund der Gerechten)*, a laborer's organization for German *emigrés* living in Paris. The lexicon and the goals of the organization were quite similar to those of the Society of the Seasons *(Société des Saisons)*, established in Paris by the revolutionaries Armand Barbes and Auguste Blanqui. One of Weitling's strongest supporters in the League was the revolutionary anti-Roman Bishop Hugues Felicité-Robert de Lamennais, whom Weitling termed a communist priest. However, the League of the Just ran afoul of the police during a riot involving both the League and Blanqui's Society. In 1839 Weitling fled to Zurich, where he met, among others, Bakunin.

Weitling's *Humanity* bore no outline of what was to become his 'system', but his second book, *The Guarantee of Harmony and Freedom, (Garantien der Harmonie und Freiheit)*, stated it completely. *The Guarantee,* published in 1842, had a considerable effect on European politics. Metternich, for one, was alarmed at such proposals as Weitling's call for top administrative posts in government to be filled by leaders of learning and science. Sitting at the top of the administrative pyramid and demanding military discipline and strict obedience was the 'Trio', representing the three branches of science: healing, physics (the laws of nature), and mechanics (machine production). Below the Trio sat the body of the highest office-holders *(Zentralmeisterkompagnie)*, who

[28]   Offered under the Russian title *Čelovečestvo, kakovo ono est' i kakovym dolžno byt'* (St. Petersburg, 1906).

would serve as a Senate and Ministry. All government functions were directed by orders issued by the very top of the pyramid.[29]

The key to Weitling's system lay in locating talented men to fill the posts. Money, ruiner of talent, was the major obstacle. Applicants for positions would be required to submit drawings, writings, and autobiographies for appraisal. Everyone would have the opportunity of a proper educational background, because a university would be established for every one million citizens. All students would be required to perform manual labor. Associations of teachers (*Lehrstand*) would make appointments in agriculture and industry.[30]

But the new society could not be born, Weitling said, except out of revolution. The proletariat must be armed to disarm the rich; partisan warfare, as Weitling had learned in the Swiss *Sonderbund* War, was an effective means of bringing transformation to society. The instability which would invariably result from this sort of social upheaval could be controlled by a caretaker revolutionary dictatorship.[31]

By 1846 Weitling was much better known among the German workers than was Karl Marx. However, his confrontation with Marx that year at Brussels destroyed him as an active force in the workers' movement. Weitling, lacking Marx's scholarly familiarity with concepts such as economic determinism, found his emotional appeals inadequate to the increasing sophistication of the movement. Also, Marx belittled Weitling's religious views, which neglected materialism in favor of a philosophy comparable to that of the Anabaptists and the Moravian Brethren.[32] In 1848, Weitling, defeated in Europe, came to the United States, where he involved himself in several small and ultimately futile workers' movements and communal experiments.

Weitling's ideas are obvious in Spešnev's plan for a secret society. He insisted, for example, on the pyramidal structure of the organization and that all orders be binding from top to bottom. Probably under Weitling's influence, he made an intensive study of primitive Christianity. Furthermore, Spešnev, like Weitling but unlike other Russian Fourierists, did not favor the right of private property, a posture which set him off from his fellow reformers in St. Petersburg. Also, only Spešnev, Černosvitov, Timkovskij, and one or two others in a halfhearted way were willing to

[29]   Carl Wittke, *The Utopian Communist: A Biography of Wilhelm Weitling, Nineteenth Century Reformer* (Baton Rouge, 1950), p. 61.
[30]   Wittke, *op. cit.*, p. 60.
[31]   V. P. Volgin, "Social'noe učenie Vejtlinga", *Voprosy istorii*, 8 (August 1961), p. 34.
[32]   Wittke, *op. cit.*, p. 109.

employ violence in social reform. But Spešnev most strongly supported Weitling's statement of the need for a secret conspiratorial organization to carry out the overthrow of a system constricted by the unjust traditions of its own past.

Nikolaj Aleksandrovič Mombelli discussed the need for a secret society, too, but Mombelli's principal desire was the formation of a Brotherhood of Mutual Aid (*Bratstvo vzaimnoj pomošči*), based on the Fourierist theme of parenthood. The Brotherhood, which Mombelli derived from Petraševskij's interpretation of the concept of association, would provide all the benefits of a family relationship without any of the faults. In simple terms, the more fortunate would help the less fortunate.

Dmitrij Dmitrievič Axšarumov pointed out an element of Fourier's teaching which had been ignored by other Russian Fourierists. He spoke of the necessity of destroying St. Petersburg and other cities and using the stone, brick, and mortar to build new homes and bring greater happiness for more people.[33] The large cities, he suggested, should be broken up into towns of 3,000 people.[34] "We Russian Fourierists", he wrote, "will begin in Russia the job of transforming our country and the whole people will finish it."[35] Axšarumov's plan contained a common flaw, however: it offered no means to its own fulfillment.

Despite that failure of practicality, Axšarumov was one of the few *Petraševcy* who offered views of the most efficacious government for Russia. He agreed with Petraševskij in calling for a republic and a constitution, but he confused his stand by using the terms president and monarch interchangeably when discussing the republic.[36] Axšarumov suggested a Ministry of Social Life (*Ministerstvo obščestvennoj žizni*) to function as a supreme economic planning board. The monarch (or president) was to have no power other than that of calling and dispersing the People's Parliament (*Narodnoe sobranie*). In this body Axšarumov located the real power of the government, directed by a prime minister. Fearing, as Petraševskij did, a dictatorial executive, he left the monarchy with no rights except that of a hereditary title.

Axšarumov was particularly vocal on two other important issues. He attacked economic conditions which made education for the children of

---

[33] Ščegolev, II, p. 192.
[34] V. I. Semevskij, "D. D. Axšarumov i A. I. Evropeus", *Golos minuvšago*, 3 (March 1916), p. 57.
[35] Ščegolev, II, p. 163.
[36] Semevskij, "Axšarumov i Evropeus", p. 67.

poor families impossible, pronouncing the continued cultural isolation of such people sinful. He also spoke out for the vital necessity of propaganda in any efforts to reform Russia. People of all walks of life must be interested in the new ideas. Libraries, he suggested, should be built and stocked with a wide variety of reading matter. On this point he found unanimous support among the Petraševcy, all of whom seemed concerned about increasing the distribution of the printed word – particularly the printed words of Fourier – across Russia. A. P. Balasoglo presented a particularly interesting scheme for achieving this end. His "Project for the Setting Up of a Book Store with a Library and Press" ("Proekt učreždenija knižnogo sklada s bibliotekoj i tipografiej"), read to the circle in 1845, called for the establishment of a low-cost central warehouse in St. Petersburg for the sale of books.[37] The store would feature specialists in charge of ordering foreign books and an adjacent library and printing press. Once the success of the first store were assured, similar establishments would be opened in other Russian cities. Balasoglo also hoped to organize a group of literary critics responsible for reporting the merits and failings of each book to the public.

Balasoglo's plan was unique in its call for the middle class to take the initiative in establishing a program which would primarily benefit them, the masses, in his opinion, not being ready for such a readership program. The entire scheme would be carried out not in the name of the government, but in the name of the people. This program was the first by a reformist group to offer a method for the dissemination of printed propaganda. Among its supporters were Apollon Nikolaevič and Valerian Nikolaevič Majkov, a wealthy guild merchant named Tatarinov, and a Ministry of Foreign Affairs archives official named Bulgakov.[38] Nevertheless, there is no record that Balasoglo made any official proposal of his program to the government.

Balasoglo's principal goal in life seemed to be the raising of Russian cultural and educational standards. His unpublished work "Notes on Art" ("Listy iskusstv") included book reviews and advertisements of the best Russian and foreign works; he also hoped to help develop a new journal. He later devised the scheme of compiling information on all textbooks, categorized by subject, into a single reference work. He went so far as to assign different categories for research by members of the Friday circle, but the scheme was never followed through.

Petraševskij shared Balasoglo's concern for Russia's low educational

---

[37] Desnitskij, op. cit., II, p. 16.
[38] Semevskij, Petraševskij i Petraševcy, II, p. 107.

and cultural standards. At the last Friday gathering, Petraševskij spoke of the importance of the social message of literature, especially that of western Europe. He stated that Russians should publish journals like those of the West. "In the West", he said, "journals are not a representation of one person but they act as an organ of transmission of all the ideas and thoughts of the social class that publishes the magazine." [39] Such a broad ideological base might be obtained by selling shares similar to those one might buy in a phalanstery to people whose ideas would then be represented by the newspaper or journal. But before publications could be improved, Petraševskij stated, Russian writers would have to overcome their educational weaknesses and inadequate understanding of the needs of society.

Even though these various schemes did not grapple directly with the problem of reform in Russia, the *Petraševcy* were more than merely utopian dreamers. Their greatest desire was for social change, and they concentrated much of their thought upon their country's main domestic problem at the time, serfdom. Just prior to the reforms which began in the 1860s, there were more than twenty-one million serfs in European Russia. There were also about nineteen million state peasants and some two million peasants living on the lands of the Imperial family. Nicholas I was more than aware of the scope of the problem. But his terrible fear of social revolution, reinforced by the Decembrist revolt, made change unthinkable to him.

Early in Nicholas' reign, in 1826, he had seen much promise in the plan of Mixail Mixailovič Speranskij, the liberal reformer under Alexander I. Speranskij had proposed that legal rights of succession on the land be granted to the peasants who farmed it. The plan, though problems of execution prevented its being carried out, reflected the thought of the reforming period of Alexander I. In 1836 Nicholas established the Fifth Section of His Imperial Majesty's Own Chancery to deal with the problems of the state peasants. Under the direction of Count P. D. Kiselev, the Chancery gained significant improvements in the lot of the state peasantry. However, little or nothing was done about the serf and his relationship with the private landlord.

A foreigner, Baron August Haxthausen, finally publicized the life of the serf in the *obščina*, or living community. In 1843 the Prussian social scientist Haxthausen toured extensively through the Russian countryside, then announced that the serf was far better off in the *obščina* than

[39]   Desnitskij, *op. cit.*, III, p. 442.

he would be if independent. Count Kiselev had anticipated Haxthausen's findings by stating earlier that instead of liquidating the *obščina*, or *mir*, the government should try to control it and work through it. In short, the regime was saying it did not dare attempt to transform the *mir*; the best it could do was enforce tighter control over it. The conservatives naturally supported Nicholas' policy, which was tantamount to burying his head in the sand. But serfdom was ruining Russia, and before the decade was out even Haxthausen was saying that "serfdom has become unnatural". Still, he argued, "the most important problem is to dissolve the relationship between the lord and serf without unleashing a social revolution".[40]

The gentry shared this terror at the thought of revolution. Their fears that the regime might very shortly be an enemy were reinforced by the 1846 revolt in Galicia, in the Habsburg Empire, in which the Vienna government backed the Ukrainian peasants against the Polish gentry. But the Russian gentry had nothing to fear from their Tsar. Nicholas personally deplored the Vienna government's action. He was opposed to any type of 'people's war' as a means to social change. Thus, although minor reforms were instituted in Poland and the southeastern territories of Russia, Nicholas refused to carry out reforms in Russia proper. With the revolution of 1848, he gave up all thought of attempting reform, and the government assumed a most reactionary stand on the question of serfdom.

The *Petraševcy* became increasingly critical of the regime's anti-reform policies.[41] Nikolaj Aleksandrovič Mombelli, in an article titled "On the Founding of Rome and the Reign of Romulus" ("Ob osnovanii Rima i carstvovanii Romula"),[42] stated that "the Roman Senate had more basis to bestow the surname 'wise' to the name of Romulus than the Russian Senate did to the name of Nicholas".[43] Romulus was concerned about the common good of his citizens, Mombelli said, but Nicholas was only interested in destroying his subjects. Mombelli pointed to the terrible condition of the peasants in Vitebsk province, many of whom had starved to death because, he charged, "all their grain had to go to the 'child-loving' Emperor (*čadoljubivyj imperator*)".

In contrast, Mombelli pointed to the countries of western Europe as

---

[40] August Haxthausen, *Studien über die inneren Zustände des Volkslebens und insbesondere die ländlichen Einrichtungen Russlands* (Hanover, 1847), I, p. 72; as quoted in Venturi, *Roots of Revolution*, p. 73.

[41] *Bol'šaja sovetskaja ènciklopedija*, second edition, XXXII (1954), p. 591.

[42] Desnitskij, *op. cit.*, I, pp. 280-289.

[43] Semevskij, *Petraševskij i Petraševcy*, II, p. 205.

more advanced than Russia; the reason, he said, was representative government and the equality of all citizens before the law in such countries as France. Only Austria had retained and strengthened the absolute form of rule. In Russia all were slaves (*raby*), but the peasants were in the most intolerable situation. Although not a Fourierist and therefore willing to use violence to accomplish reform, Mombelli offered no specific plan for the emancipation of the serfs.

As one of Russia's early economists, V. A. Miljutin was one of the first Russians to point out the economic disadvantages of serfdom. His theories seem to have been chiefly influenced by two French writers, Francis Vidal and Jean Charles Leonard Simonde de Sismondi. Miljutin's critical analysis of impoverishment and pauperism in the West[44] bears the mark of Vidal's influence. Vidal, a socialist but not a revolutionary, wrote *De la répartition des richesses* (1846) to expose the terrible antagonisms which he saw developing between the classes in western Europe. Although he contended that a reconstruction of society could be carried out only by the central government, Vidal was candid in forecasting a social war between the classes.[45]

Miljutin's writings on the agrarian situation in France and England may have been influenced by Sismondi, whose principle work *Nouveaux principes d'économie politique, ou de la richesse dans ses rapports avec la population (New Principles of Political Economy, or Wealth in Its Relationship to the Population)* was published in 1819.[46] Prior to Vidal, Sismondi had postulated that "only the government could break down the inequalities in society".[47] Miljutin agreed with Sismondi's charge that 'economic science' spent too much time studying the means to increase wealth and too little time studying means by which wealth might produce greater happiness. He also approved Sismondi's criticism of Adam Smith "for not having the riches shared by all the people".[48]

But Miljutin faulted Sismondi for not seeing that a radical social transformation was the only cure for economic ills which plagued the West. Miljutin had written of such a transformation in Russia, but the censor had forced him to delete discussion of his methods.[49] Like Petraševskij, Miljutin was no revolutionary; he hoped that violence would

---

[44] *Èpoxa feodalizma: Čast' vtoraja, 1800-1861*, ed. A. I. Paškov = Vol. I of *Istorija russkoj èkonomičeskoj mysli* (Moscow, 1958), p. 339.
[45] Francis Vidal, *De la répartition des richesses* (Paris, 1846), p. 173.
[46] Third edition, 2 volumes (Geneva, 1951-1953).
[47] *Nouveaux principes*, I.
[48] *Nouveaux principes*, I, p. 41.
[49] Makašin, *Saltykov-Ščedrin*, I, p. 227.

not be necessary for change. He hoped that an enlightened government (*prosveščennoe pravitel'stvo*) would rule over and above the classes and that a reconstruction of society could then take place. He opted for a "gradual amelioration" (*postepennoe soveršenstvovanie*) rather than "great leaps forward" so that necessary preparation could precede change. In articles in *Otečestvennye zapiski* and the *Sovremennik* in 1847, Miljutin came out for a peaceful, not a revolutionary social transformation. However, he stated a grave warning: "If Russia doesn't begin to make changes on her economy, the ulcer of poverty and suffering in the society from economic dislocations will grow terrible." [50]

Miljutin's economic critique pointed to the root cause of Russia's problems: serfdom. But when he put the question into the larger framework of political economy, he devised a criticism of capitalism. Russia's problems, he said, could never be solved by capitalistic means, only through socialism. Furthermore, Miljutin said, serfdom was more than a social problem, for social and political problems were inseparable. Unfortunately, Miljutin stopped attending Petraševskij's Fridays before the discussions of reform, which took place in 1848-1849, began, so there is no record of his suggesting means for freeing the serfs.

Another *Petraševec* who disagreed with the economic philosophy of Adam Smith was I. L. Jastžembskij, who felt that the evil of *laissez-faire* lay in the fact that so few people were allowed to participate in the riches of society. [51] As a result, Jastžembskij felt, the working class has been turned into cattle (*skot*). Since it was plain that unlimited competition was going to destroy the western world, socialism, and in particular Fourierism, was the answer to Russia's difficulties. But, unlike Miljutin, Jastžembskij saw no weakness in Sismondi's theory; he did not arrive at the point where violence was the only means to social transformation and socialism in the West.

V. A. Golovinskij disputed the whole idea of government emancipation of the serfs, arguing that the serf was better off in servitude and with land than he would be free and without land. It was obvious to Golovinskij that the Tsar would never give the freed serfs land; he foresaw the possibility, therefore, of a peasant uprising. [52] Petraševskij, greatly disturbed by the prospect of a peasant revolt and class warfare, argued against Golovinskij that reform of the judicial system was a more im-

---

[50] Miljutin, *op. cit.*, pp. 353-354.
[51] V. I. Semevskij, "Propaganda Petraševcev v učebnyx zavedenijax", *Golos minuvšago*, 2 (February 1917), p. 140.
[52] Ščegolev, *op. cit.*, III, p. 203.

portant issue than emancipation because the "courts affected the lives of almost sixty million people", which was then the entire population of the country.[53] Petraševskij also demanded the introduction of a jury system into Russia, contending that the jury would represent the people and not the regime. While most of the *Petraševcy* accepted Petraševskij's enunciation of the order of the sequence of reforms, Axšarumov felt that judicial reform and emancipation of the serfs should come the same day.[54]

The *Petraševcy* surveyed the impact of the revolutions of 1848 on reform in Russia with divided opinions. Some – including Spešnev, Timkovskij, and Černosvitov – thought that with the tension in Europe the government could not begin any reforms that would not be construed as appeasement.[55] Petraševskij suggested that parallels were fallacious: the Russian people would not follow the revolutionary lead of their European neighbors. They no longer believed in a new Pugačev and would wait patiently for emancipation by the supreme authority.[56]

But emancipation would come, most of the *Petraševcy* felt, and several plans were advanced in preparation for the day. P. N. Filippov, Dostoevskij's friend, proposed a 'going out to the gentry' (*xoždenie v dvorjanstvo*) to impress upon them the need for emancipation. He was convinced that the gentry would readily consent to abandoning serfdom once they understood its evils.[57] But Filippov's idea found little support among the *Petraševcy*, possibly because so many of them were of gentry background.

Golovinskij, however, agreed with certain aspects of Filippov's suggestion. He said that emancipation of the serfs might take one of two roads. The more desirable would involve an agreement between the gentry and the peasants in each province, followed by a request that the government carry out the agreed upon reforms. Golovinskij recognized that class egotism, self-love and an ignorance of economic problems would constitute sizeable obstacles on this road.[58]

The second alternative was emancipation from above. But Golovinskij anticipated the question of whether the autocracy, the highest law, dedicated in normal times to preserving the existing inter-class

[53] Desnitskij, *op. cit.*, III, p. 425.
[54] V. I. Semevskij, *Krest'janskij vopros v Rossii v XVIII i v pervoj polovine XIX veka*, II (St. Petersburg, 1888), p. 379.
[55] Semevskij, *Krest'janskij vopros*, II, p. 380.
[56] Semevskij, *Krest'janskij vopros*, II, p. 381.
[57] Bel'čikov, *op. cit.*, p. 37.
[58] Lejkina, *op. cit.*, p. 35.

relationship, could maintain the balance of power once it had upset the apple cart by freeing the serfs. Under the best of circumstances, Golovinskij decided, it might be necessary to impose a temporary dictatorship while the reforms were being carried out.[59]

The *Petraševcy* worked actively to promote the concept of reform among the townspeople. For example, they conversed with cabdrivers and tried to harden them against the owners and the government.[60] The informer Antonelly accused Jastžembskij of telling one coachman "not to pay his taxes to the government agent but to give him a blow on the head". Jastžembskij went on to ask the driver if the German anti-Christ landlord took quit rents. If he did not, why did the serf allow a landlord of the Orthodox faith to drag it out of the Russian peasant? Jastžembskij concluded that even if the gentry wanted to free the serfs the Tsar would never permit it.[61]

Privately, many members of the government were quick to admit the iniquities of serfdom, but publicly the regime permitted no criticism of it. For example, Filippov charged that the gentry was in violation of the Ten Commandments in making the peasants gather hay even on Sunday.[62] Filippov, a devout believer, warned that such injustices would bring retribution both from God and from the Tsar down on the heads of the landlords. But the government prosecutor later labeled Filippov's speech seditious because it upset the official thinking of a regime which would not allow spoken that which it did not wish to hear.

Beklemišev felt a particular urgency attached to the question of emancipation of the serfs. Apparently, rumors were flying that the Tsar wanted emancipation but that the gentry would not permit it, rumors which Beklemišev described as "the idea of freedom, like an electric spark . . . racing through the villages".[63] The good will of the gentry was necessary, he said, if revolt was to be forestalled. The peasants could not be freed without land, of course, or the gentry would become responsible for their welfare. Moreover, a free but unlanded peasantry would soon become frustrated and turn to drunkenness and murdering their landlords. Beklemišev's plan for avoiding this sort of unpleasantness called for the lords to grant freedom and land to the serfs immediately.

59   Lejkina, *op. cit.*, p. 36.
60   Semevskij, *Krest'janskij vopros*, II, p. 380.
61   Semevskij, *Krest'janskij vopros*, II, p. 381.
62   Evgrafov, *op. cit.*, pp. 637-645.
63   Desnitskij, *op. cit.*, II, p. 394.

The novelty of Beklemišev's scheme lay in his plan for building a local school for each three hundred peasants through the "common effort of the gentry and the peasants",[64] the former supplying the capital and the latter the labor. Teachers would be selected by a commission on which district chiefs, district school superintendents and priests would sit. A combination of salary from the students and land contributed by landlords and peasants would make up the teachers' pay.

The core of Beklemišev's plan was a sense of responsibility on the part of the gentry, without which social improvements were impossible. Urgency was essential, Beklemišev warned, because the peasants had already waited too long.

A certain helplessness may be detected in the writing and speaking of the *Petraševcy* on the subject of serfdom. They were convinced that the institution must be abolished, but they did not know how it could be done. Petraševskij in particular was guided in his thinking by Fourier, who, having seen the French Revolution, had been convinced that violence and terror never accomplished anything positive. Reform, Petraševskij stated, must come through legal means, not through a corroding, dehumanizing revolution. He hoped that a spirit of providentialism, of mutual respect (as Petr Čaadaev used it), would develop in the lower classes to prepare them for the personal liberty they would enjoy after the great reform. He suggested legally encouraging the gentry to sell lands to the merchant class, thereby breaking down traditional class barriers.

On the other hand, the left wing of the *Petraševcy*, made up of Spešnev, Timkovskij, and Černosvitov, was not articulate in its efforts to foment an upheaval. These three lacked experience, had no real leadership, and, in effect, were unable to move their planning beyond the talking stage. Černosvitov was a member of the circle for such a short time (he returned to Siberia in January of 1849) that he never had a chance to incite much conspiratorial fervor among the *Petraševcy*.

The Populist approach of Beklemišev and others had no real chance for success because the gentry was not willing to surrender its rights without a fight. If the government had sanctioned the idea of educating the landlords in their responsibilities to the peasants after emancipation, things might have been different. But of course Nicholas' regime would brook no change in the social structure of the country, so even

---

[64]   Desnitskij, *op. cit.,* **II, p. 395.**

Beklemišev's plan, the most positive to come out of the group, was never executed.

Although they were keenly influenced by certain western European philosophers, the *Petraševcy* made no original contribution to nineteenth century religious thought. As noted earlier, Petraševskij was enamored of Saint-Simon's "New Christianity"; Weitling's influence brought with it the concept of a return to primitive Christianity. Bishop Lamennais' *Paroles d'un Croyant (Words of a Believer)* struck them with its demand for "the end of all despotism and substitution of the rule of justice and charity",[65] and with its call for a return to the simplicity of primitive Christianity. But Lamennais' work contained a strong social note, an unshakable belief in progress as the means to a better social order. He wrote of the voice of the people, and of its expression through public opinion and the ballot box, as the agent for bringing God's reign on earth. The *Petraševcy* received as leading tenets of their philosophy his theories along with Saint-Simon's idea that "all society must work to ameliorate the moral and physical existence of the poor class and to do this the society must organize".[66]

Ludwig Feuerbach's interpretation of the social aspect of Christianity was explained to the group by Feliks G. Tol'. Tol' said that God and religion were found in nature and that man was driven to God by fear. Feuerbach had written of the subject-object relationship of man and God. Man is determined by air around him, but when man scientifically analyzes air he changes the relationship. Similarly, Feuerbach said, the man who is determined by the will of those around him has no independent will of his own. Only the thinker, the analyzer, is free and independent. It is through understanding that man reduces the things around him to mere means of his own existence,[67] and this man must do if he is to be more than the means for another human being. Also, as Tol' reported, Feuerbach postulated that man cannot survive in isolation; his natural creativity can only develop in association with others.[68]

The *Petraševcy* saw Feuerbach's theories as a weapon against the organized support which Russian Orthodoxy lent to the Tsar's absolutist

[65]   Charles Pearson, *The Politico-Social Ideas of Lamennais* (New York, 1936), p. 3.
[66]   Claude Henri de Saint-Simon, *Nouveau Christianisme* (Paris, 1832), p. 85.
[67]   Ludwig Andreas Feuerbach, *The Essence of Christianity*, translated by Marian Evans from the seventh German edition (New York, 1855), p. 63.
[68]   Feuerbach, *op. cit.*, p. 118.

government. They also liked David Friedrich Strauss's *The Life of Jesus*, which attempted to explain the miracles of Jesus rationally.[69] The social ethics of Christianity appealed to all the *Petraševcy*, even those who proclaimed themselves atheists.

From these various sources, then, Petraševskij and his colleagues compiled a sincere social conscience that drove them to demand radical reforms for the benefit of all Russians. For most of them, discussion of and planning for social and political change was the *raison d'être* of the circle. In their heat of commitment, however, they were helpless to devise workable plans for change and the means for executing them. Frustration led to the formation of a conspiracy within their ranks, which in turn contributed to their eventual downfall.

[69]   David Friedrich Strauss, *The Life of Jesus*, trans. Marian Evans (New York, 1856).

VII

CONSPIRATORIAL ORGANIZATION

Chief among the ironies involved in the affairs of the Petraševskij Circle is the fact that the government's greatest fear of the group was the least substantial element of the *Petraševcy* character. The Investigating Commission which took testimony from the *Petraševcy* following their arrest in 1849 focused most intensely on the existence of a secret conspiratorial society which was dedicated to the forceful overthrow of the regime. But due to the nature of the Circle and its leaders' penchant for disagreement among themselves, a working conspiracy was the least likely product of the Friday meetings.

Nikolaj Aleksandrovič Spešnev was first considered by the Commission to be the Circle's most dangerous revolutionary. Spešnev made no bones about his loathing for the government of Nicholas I. When he returned to St. Petersburg from travels in western Europe in 1847, he told his intimates of his new awareness that Socialism was not a new form of political economy but a new form of politics.[1] Although he believed in a Socialist economy, he declared no allegiance to a particular form of Socialism. He certainly was no Fourierist, for Fourierism provided no means for the overthrow of the Tsar. Spešnev basically stated two Socialist goals: the nationalization of agriculture and industry and the forcible transformation of the existing order in Russia. Toward achieving these goals, he urged the formation of a secret society.

However, it was Mombelli's "Brotherhood of Mutual Aid" scheme which constituted the group's most feasible plan for a secret organization, an estimation reinforced by the fact that the Investigating Commission spent more time probing the Brotherhood than any other topic. Mombelli first discussed his scheme with L'vov in private meetings taking place in 1848. Mombelli pointed out that the indiviual ego was the source of all of man's problems. Because man loves himself so

---

[1] V. R. Lejkina, *Petraševcy* (Moscow, 1924), p. 40.

much, he said, "the ideal love is only temporary and cannot last long enough".[2] The family unit constitutes the ideal relationship among people, but it is an unrealized ideal in most cases because even kinfolk live separate lives. By Mombelli's interpretation, a young man soon discovers that family love is not what he has imagined it is; he then becomes hardened toward society in general and ends up a callous egoist in love only with himself.

As an adaptation of the family unit ideal, however, the Brotherhood would be a means toward a better society. Mombelli described the Brotherhood as offering family benefits without family faults. "All the brothers would help each other in material ways but chiefly in moral ways", he said.[3] A weak-willed person might fall in the mud if left on his own but not with the Brotherhood to guide and support his steps. Among other achievements of the Brotherhood would be the curing of alcoholics and beggars.

The Brotherhood plan, based on the notion of individual human progress, was nevertheless an associational scheme for social improvement. This aspect of it appealed immediately to Petraševskij's love of any association.[4] Petraševskij was generally ambivalent about the use of revolutionary force, but he was unreserved in his praise of Mombelli's plan as a vehicle for spreading truth, enlightenment, education, and social transformation. He agreed with Mombelli that propaganda was the most useful device for instituting the Brotherhood throughout Russia.

After Mombelli had discussed his plan with L'vov and Petraševskij, the three decided to invite Spešnev to join them. They later also invited Konstantin Debu, although, as a fanatical Fourierist, Debu added little to the conversations. The proposed society was never discussed among the Petraševcy at the Friday gatherings, but the five supporters of the Brotherhood idea met between four and six times at Spešnev's house in late 1848 and January, 1849. As they argued the objectives of the society, Spešnev suggested that the abolition of serfdom be one of their chief aims, although he failed to elaborate on the means to this end. Everyone agreed with Petraševskij's idea that the society could be used as a propaganda vehicle, although Mombelli disagreed with him later on the question of setting up a Scientific Committee (*Učenyj komitet*) to consider all social issues on a scientific basis. Petraševskij's proposal that all future members be admitted to the society on the basis of auto-

[2] V. A. Desnitskij (ed.), *Delo Petraševcev*, I (Moscow, 1937), p. 349.
[3] Desnitskij, *op. cit.*, I, p. 350.
[4] Desnitskij, *op. cit.*, I, p. 107.

biographical statements showing individual evolutionary development, or progress, was soundly defeated by his four colleagues, who felt that such a device was totally unnecessary.[5]

The planning of the Brotherhood never got beyond the first stages because of the violent clashes between Petraševskij and Spešnev on the question of objectives. Spešnev wanted a secret conspiratorial society with the avowed aim of overthrowing the existing order. He insisted on laying the power to make binding decisions in the hands of a political organization which could work for as long as ten years to prepare the way for revolution. Instead of a study group such as Petraševskij's Scientific Committee, Spešnev proposed a Central Committee (*central'nyj komitet*) made up of people who represented the various shades of opinion in the country. A separate subcommittee would be set up to represent each of these different viewpoints. But all decisions from top to bottom would be subordinated to the control of the Central Committee; strict discipline would be maintained.

One of the group proposed that the five of them act as a Central Committee with the powers indicated in Spešnev's plan. There would be a central bank and a treasurer responsible for collecting monthly dues; the money was to be used to help the less fortunate get on their feet. Someone also suggested that each of the five invite one new member to join the society. But eventually all their plans fell into disarray: Mombelli rejected Spešnev's vision of a political Brotherhood and although Petraševskij tried to revive the original scheme, Spešnev washed his hands of the whole affair.

As in other matters, Petraševskij's views on violent revolution tended toward the contradictory. While he was opposed to the general notion of revolution as a means to social change, he became involved in plans for stirring up tribes on the periphery of Russia and thereby embarrassing the regime into reform. The informer, Antonelli, had claimed to have influence with some Cherkas tribesmen who were living in St. Petersburg. Petraševskij instructed Antonelli to 'enlighten' the mountaineers about their actual status. "They must be able to understand", he told Antonelli, "that through their subordination to the Tsarist government they [have] lost their independence." Control of the Cherkas trade was not in the tribe's hands, he pointed out, but in Russian hands. If the Cherkas could be incited to overthrow the Tsarist power in the Caucasus, the resulting necessity for the government to conscript

---

[5] Desnitskij, *op. cit.*, I, p. 352.

troops and raise taxes would inflame public opinion throughout Russia proper.

Antonelli at this point claimed that the plan would not work because it was impossible to get the Cherkas tribesman to understand what their rights were.[6] On the other hand, both Petraševskij and Mombelli reported excellent opportunities for revolt in the Ukraine, in Volhynia, in Podolia and in the region around Kiev.

Mombelli during this time was in correspondence with Taras Grigorievič Ševčenko, who was strongly influential in the Cyril and Methodius Society in 1846.[7] The goals of the Society included the creation of a Slavic democratic confederation headquartered at Kiev and, more important to the Petraševskij Circle, the abolition of serfdom and gentry privileges. Like the *Petraševcy*, the Cyril and Methodius Society was split by disagreement over the use of force to achieve its goals. Interestingly, Petraševskij favored in the Society's program those same revolutionary aspirations which he deplored among the *Petraševcy*. But chronicles of the Society up to the time of its disbanding by the police in April, 1847, disclose that while it and the Petraševskij Circle were aware of one another's existence, no conspiratorial link was ever forged between them.

The specter of a wide-spread secret organization loomed again in the informer Antonelli's report that the *Petraševcy* had established a number of secret contacts inside Russia. One of those alleged contacts was with Ivan Afanas'evič Romašev, who in 1846 was an inspector of the district school in Gdov. Romašev was supposed to belong to a Kharkov society organized with "the goal of changing the form of government among the Slavic race". To this 'society' belonged Petraševskij and possibly other *Petraševcy*. Romašev's project, calling for the establishment of a Republican constitution for Russia, came to the attention of the police when he sent a copy of it to the leader of the gentry in the Gdov district, who promptly denounced him to the authorities. Romašev was arrested in October of 1846 and sat in the Schlüsselburg prison until 1867, denying all the while that he had ever heard of Mixail Petraševskij.[8]

In the fall of 1848, a new figure appeared at the Friday gatherings. He was Konstantin Ivanovič Timkovskij, a government official from

---

[6] Desnitskij, *op. cit.*, III, p. 385.
[7] V. R. Lejkina-Svirskaja, *Petraševcy* (Moscow, 1965), p. 111.
[8] V. I. Semevskij, *Sobranie sočinenij: M. V. Butaševič-Petraševskij i Petraševcy*, ed. V. V. Vodovozov, II (Moscow, 1922), p. 182.

Revel' and a diligent student of Fourier. Petraševskij doubted the sincerity of Timkovskij's devotion to Fourierism and refused to let him speak at the Fridays, so he gave talks at Spešnev's house. Debu reported that in his first talk Timkovskij came out against the revolution. But F. G. Tol' quoted Timkovskij as saying that "he wanted to see an insurrection on the square" before he returned to Revel'.[9] Comparing "himself to Samson", Timkovskij declared that he was ready to go out "on the square" himself. He outlined a plan calling for many Fourierist circles throughout Russia, with mutual coordination maintained by having the leaders of the circles meet occasionally for discussions.[10]

Many Petraševcy were terrified by Timskovskij's speech about "going out on the square". Until his arrival, there had been no open talk of revolution. To most of them, he remained an enigma; some even thought he was a spy. Although only his brother Aleksej and Spešnev gave Timkovskij's ideas their unqualified support, seven Petraševcy attended a dinner in his honor to indicate that their thoughts were similar to his. Petraševskij was conspicuously absent, having declined an invitation.

At the trial of the Petraševcy, the government accused Timkovskij of having advocated a division of the world between the communists and the Fourierists. The charge was based upon correspondence between Timkovskij and Petraševskij which has since been lost. The only remnant is a scratch copy of a letter in which Petraševskij scolded Timkovskij for being a neophyte.

Upon his return to Revel', Timkovskij attempted to spread the ideas of Fourier among his neighbors. He wrote to Spešnev claiming to have organized two Fourierist circles. It appears, however, that Spešnev lost interest in him and that nothing more was heard about him until he was arrested in April, 1849, with the other Petraševcy.

There were other Fourierist study groups in Russia in the mid-1840s. The brothers Beketovyj – Aleksej, Nikolaj, and Andrej – led a circle in St. Petersburg, but their only link with the Petraševcy was Dostoevskij's brief attendance of their meeting.[11] In 1846 the Beketovyj brothers moved to Kazan', as did the Blagoveščenskijs, another St. Petersburg family interested in Fourierism and Socialism. The groups led by these two families in Kazan' apparently discussed the works of various Socialist writers of western Europe and are distinguished primarily by the

⁹   Semevskij, Petraševskij i Petraševcy, II, p. 125.
¹⁰ Semevskij, Petraševskij i Petraševcy, II, p. 126.
¹¹ Lejkina-Svirskaja, Petraševcy (1965), p. 16.

fact that one of their members was an 1847 graduate of the University of Kazan' named Lev Nicolaevič Tolstoj.

Vladimir Ivanovič Kajdanov was an official of the Ministry of State Domains stationed in Rostov in Jaroslav province. Through correspondence with his brother Nikolaj, a *Petraševec*, Kajdanov attempted to start a Fourierist circle.[12] However, there is no evidence that the groups in Jaroslav, Revel, Kazan or St. Petersburg ever produced anything resembling a secret conspiratorial organization.

In November of 1848, another new visitor to the Friday meetings at Petraševskij's house stirred considerable interest. Rafail Aleksandrovič Černosvitov was a widely traveled man whose scope of view deeply impressed the *Petraševcy*. "Among the *Petraševcy*, city dwellers and intellectuals, Černosvitov appeared as a man of strong will."[13] He and Spešnev were the only members of the group who had actually seen revolution. Spešnev had been involved in the Swiss *Sonderbund* War; Černosvitov had participated in the suppression of peasant revolts. Černosvitov also knew more than any of the *Petraševcy* about the land and the people of the Urals. He was familiar with the economic and social conditions in which the peasants and factory workers of eastern Russia lived. His involvement in gold mining in Siberia had given him first-hand knowledge of the working conditions of miners. He made a lasting impression on many of the *Petraševcy*, particularly Spešnev.

After Černosvitov's first visit, Petraševskij took him aside and listened to his remarks. Černosvitov told Petraševskij and Spešnev about the peasant revolts in Perm' province,[14] from which he had learned that when government forces showed the slightest hesitation the peasants fought even more fiercely. Spešnev's questions came in a barrage; he was beginning to see a method for inciting revolution all over Russia. If a peasant revolt could be controlled, he figured, the leaders could make of it what they wanted. He began to envision a new Pugačev revolt spreading to the cities and overturning and transforming all of society. Spešnev thought it highly significant that the most restless peasantry, by Černosvitov's report, was in the Urals, the spawning ground of the Pugačev rebellion.

Other than Timkovskij, no *Petraševec* had spoken openly in support

---

[12] Lejkina, *Petraševcy* (1924), p. 118.
[13] Lejkina, *op. cit.*, p. 47.
[14] For treatment of these peasant disturbances, see M. S. Valevskij, "Volnenija krest'jan v zaural'skoj časti Permskogo kraja v 1842-1843", *Russkaja starina*, 11, 12, I (November, December 1879), pp. 411-432, 627-646.

of armed revolt. But now there was Černosvitov, striking a chord in the *Petraševcy* with a plan for uprising. Revolution could be incited in eastern Siberia, he said, if an army corps could be sent to aid the insurgents. Once the revolt had crossed the Urals, it would be joined by 100,000 factory workers. It would then flow along the Don River, drawing the Cossacks into its ranks. The regime would be forced to meet the rising tide with extra troops, leaving opportunities for simultaneous revolts to break out in St. Petersburg and Moscow. Such a detailed strategy, however, would take at least five years to prepare and would require a strong secret organization.

The discussion of such a secret organization caused a dispute between Petraševskij and Spešnev from which their friendship never recovered. Petraševskij denied under Černosvitov's questioning that such a secret society did, or in fact even should, exist among the *Petraševcy*. Spešnev argued for the creation of such a society, stating that he favored communism over Fourierism and that he was not afraid to use force and violence to achieve social transformation. Petraševskij countered that an uprising was unnecessary and that "in order to attain the goal of a new society it was necessary to rely on the law and legal forms as much as possible".[15] Spešnev stalked out and did not return to Petraševskij's for a short while.

Černosvitov left St. Petersburg soon after and returned to Siberia. But his presence had been felt among the *Petraševcy*, and in the last six months of the circle's existence there was increasing agitation from some of the members to form a conspiratorial society. Černosvitov had explained to them how the peasants could be used to create revolution, a new concept. From the time of Černosvitov's departure until the arrests in April, 1849, the *Petraševcy* saw more clearly the correlation between the question of the secret society and the problem of serf emancipation.

In final analysis, though, there is no substantial evidence that a secret conspiratorial organization was ever formed among the *Petraševcy*. The Investigating Commission took considerable testimony on the matter and even they concluded that Spešnev, the most obvious suspect in the hunt for leaders of such an organization, was nothing more than a whimsical, posturing playboy acting out a cloak-and-dagger role among his former Lyceum classmates – a conclusion which resulted from Spešnev's application of charm and heretofore unrealized acting ability during his appearance before the Commissioners.[16] In retrospect, it

---

[15]　Lejkina (1924), p. 50.
[16]　Lejkina, *op. cit.*, pp. 41-42.

appears that the *Petraševcy* who favored such a society were handi-capped by lack of time to develop an organization, serious doubts as to the objectives of such an organization and a frustrating shortage of organizational ability among the principals involved. So despite the fact that the *Petraševcy* were made up of, and counseled by, individuals with sufficient intellectualism, idealism, and experience to foment a quite possibly successful revolution, a truly purposeful conspiracy never came into being.

VIII

THE ARREST, INVESTIGATION AND PUNISHMENT OF
THE *PETRAŠEVCY*

Even though their internecine squabbling prevented the *Petraševcy* from
leading social reform in Russia, their efforts did not go entirely unnoticed in all quarters. The Ministry of the Interior had first taken an
interest in Mixail Petraševskij in January, 1848, when it received a
lithographed copy of his tract "A Method to Increase the Value of
Landed Estates". Petraševskij was placed under surveillance, but no
immediate action was taken against him because the views expressed
in the tract were commonly held by many in intelligentsia circles. In
fact, if it had not been for a particular combination of international and
domestic circumstances at the time, the affair of the *Petraševcy* might
have been forgotten by the government.

But since 1843 there had been a running feud in progress between
Count Aleksej Orlov, head of the Third Section, and Lev Alekseevič
Perovskij, the Minister of the Interior and Orlov's rival for the Tsar's
favor. In March of 1848, Perovskij had ordered General Ivan Liprandi,
a Ministry expert on anti-government dissenters, to undertake full-scale
surveillance of the entire Petraševskij circle. Perovskij was determined
to prove to Nicholas the existence of a huge criminal element, including
subversives, in St. Petersburg. Orlov scoffed at the idea, maintaining
that there was absolutely nothing dangerous about the *Petraševcy*.

But events taking place outside Russia were inflating Nicholas' fear
of any internal dissent to his regime. In February, 1848, there was
another revolution in France. Each succeeding month brought fresh
news of the spread of revolt and liberalism across western Europe.
Nicholas became increasingly agitated and more determined that there
must be no opportunity for a repetition of the revolt that had welcomed
him to the throne in 1825. He listened to Perovskij, encouraging him to
maintain his surveillance of the *Petraševcy*. By early April, Orlov had
detected the depth of Nicholas' wrath against Petraševskij, whom he
considered a traitor to his class, and the *Petraševcy*; Orlov changed his

tune, telling the Tsar that the case was in fact quite dangerous and that only the Third Section could handle it effectively.

Meanwhile, a rumor spread around the city that the Tsar was to be assassinated at a masquerade ball on the night of April 21. There were reports that a lottery was to be held in the hall of the Assembly of Nobles and that the admission tickets carried printed instructions for the uprising.[1] On the body of a dead officer was found a plan pinpointing the locations of barricades in the streets of St. Petersburg. To this discovery the Tsar responded, "The beasts not only want to kill me, but my whole family."[2] While causing a great stir within the government, however, these stories were never published in the official papers; the Tsar insisted that the inflammatory rumors be squelched.

On April 21, Orlov received Nicholas' approval of his plan for the arrest of the *Petraševcy*. They were to be rounded up on the night of either April 22 or 23 and taken with their personal papers to Third Section headquarters. In all, there were thirty-four arrest orders signed by the Tsar's own hand.[3] Orlov had seven others on his list, but at the time he did not know their whereabouts.

On the night of April 22, the carriage being sent for the *Petraševcy* left Third Section headquarters. Perovskij, furious about Orlov's soldiers being allowed to stage the arrests when his Ministry had done all the painstaking investigative work, sent General Liprandi along in the carriage with General Leontij Vasil'evič Dubel't, Orlov's representative. A feared ice break-up on the Neva which could have disrupted communications necessary to the seizures never developed, and the *Petraševcy* were taken completely by surprise.[4]

Liprandi and Dubel't arrived together at Petraševskij's house on Pokrovskaja Square. Because they expected to catch a number of *Petraševcy* there, Liprandi allowed his military colleague "the risk of going up to Petraševskij's apartment while he remained hidden in the carriage".[5] When the soldiers entered the apartment and awakened Petraševskij, he reacted characteristically. Told by Dubel't to get dressed, he replied that he would go in the night clothes he was wearing. He relented only when told that he would be questioned by some very high officials. As Petraševskij changed, Dubel't, taking notes on the young

[1] P. E. Ščegolev (ed.), *Petraševcy*, I (Moscow, 1926), p. 95.
[2] Ščegolev, *op. cit.*, I, p. 95.
[3] M. O. Geršenzon (ed.), *Russkaja byl': Èpoxa Nikolaja I*, VII (Moscow, 1910), p. 168.
[4] Geršenzon, *op. cit.*, VII, p. 167.
[5] See Ščegolev, *Petraševcy*, I, p. 93.

radical's library, asked why there were so many officially forbidden books on his shelves. Reading, Petraševskij answered, was "a matter of taste".[6]

Orlov's raiding party arrived at Dostoevskij's house at four-thirty in the morning. They demanded not only his person, but all his books and papers as well. By Dostoevskij's own account, they made a thorough search. "A policeman climbed onto the table", Dostoevskij reported, "and then on top of the stove. But he lost his balance and fell off the stove; only then were the police satisfied that there was nothing important on the stove."[7] He was taken in the carriage to the Third Section, where he joined the other *Petraševcy* in standing around outside the building under the eyes of guards who had no idea what to do with them.

An official appeared with a list of names, the first of which was Antonelli's. When the clustered prisoners saw the word "agent" next to Antonelli's name, they cried out in disgust. Now they knew who had done them in! Their rancor at discovering who the spy was later was exemplified in the *Petraševec* Petr Ivanovič Beletskij, who, upon his release less than three months after his arrest, met Antonelli on the street and punched him. For that assault, Beletskij was sentenced to Vologda for four years.

Finally Dubel't appeared to take charge of the prisoners. They were processed and jailed, but they still were not informed of the reason for their arrest. Such a formality as citing the charges against them would have little difference, actually, for in the eyes of the regime they were every one guilty. If they had been innocent, they would not have been arrested; each man's degree of guilt was all that was left to be determined.

The next day, April 23, Nicholas set up a commission to investigate the affair. The commandant of the Peter and Paul Fortress, where the *Petraševcy* were held, Ivan Aleksandrovič Nabokov, was titular chairman of the commission; but Pavel Pavlovič Gagarin, a State Council member, held the power. Others seated on the panel were Prince Vasilij Dolgorukov, General Dubel't and Jakov Ivanovič Rostovcev, Commandant of the Russian Military Schools and Durov's uncle. So the commission represented the army and the Third Section,[8] with Orlov acting as interrogator and as liaison between the commission and the Tsar.

The Gagarin Commission, as the body was called, had at its disposal literally volumes of *Petraševcy* book lists, personal papers and corre-

[6]   Ščegolev, *op. cit.*, I, p. 84.
[7]   Ščegolev, *op. cit.*, I, p. 166.
[8]   U. A. Desnitskij (ed.), "Predislovie", *Delo Petraševcev*, I (Moscow, 1941), xviii.

spondence. There were sheafs of reports from Antonelli, including three lists of visitors to Petraševskij's house. General Liprandi's surveillance had yielded forty reports. Within two days, Orlov was convinced that the five-man Commission would be unable to deal with so much material. Thus on April 26 an auxiliary commission under State Secretary Prince Golicyn, one of the most powerful men in Russia at the time, was established to handle the papers of the most important *Petraševcy*.

With little to work with but the 'unsubstantiated' reports of the government agents, the Gagarin Commission devoted its time to oral examination of the lesser *Petraševcy* – a group in which Spešnev was initially placed – and the infrequent visitors to the Fridays. The questioning began five days after the arrests. The Gagarin Commission heard oral testimony, read testimony drafted by the prisoners in their cells and heard excerpts from the spies' reports. By May 4, the Golicyn panel had reviewed the papers of Petraševskij, Tol', and Jastžembskij, who were then considered the most influential members of the circle. These papers were then turned over to the Gagarin Commission.

Testimony taken from those arrested first led to the seizure of other *Petraševcy*, as ordered by the Gagarin Commission. Between April and September, a total of 252 people were brought in for questioning, although 158 of them were released.[9] The material evidence – preliminary testimony, personal papers, etc. – increased in volume with the number of arrests made. The Commission submitted specific written questions to the prisoners, who wrote in their cells answers to queries about their personal beliefs, general attitudes toward life, their opinions of other *Petraševcy* and their individual degrees of complicity in the affair. By May 31, the Commission could begin to compile a document from excerpts from the reams of written testimony.

The first evidence of 'subversion' turned up on May 18 when the Commission discovered the speech Timkovskij gave in the fall of 1848 and Beklemišev's "Correspondence Between Two Landowners". Agents were dispatched to Revel' to arrest both of them. But the bombshell burst on May 20 when Golicyn sent Spešnev's papers to the Gagarin Commission. In those papers the investigators discovered Spešnev's plan for the organization of a secret society and his promise to participate in an uprising. In Timkovskij's letters to Spešnev, the Commission learned of Timkovskij's attempt to form a secret Fourierist society in Revel'. There were also references to Grigor'ev's "A Conversation among Soldiers" and a mention of N. Ja. Danilevskij; within a week

[9] V. R. Lejkina-Svirskaja, *Petraševcy* (Moscow, 1965), p. 143.

Danilevskij was arrested while on a business trip to the south of Russia.

A new dimension had been added to the investigation. The Commission was thrown into shocked confusion; Nicholas ordered a swift and satisfactory conclusion to the whole business. Dubel't stated that Spešnev was a worse offender even than Petraševskij.[10] The regime showed its new respect for the liberal young gentryman by fitting him with fetters for his legs.

The government was even more startled on the twenty-fourth by the contents of Mombelli's papers, which included his proposed "Brotherhood of Mutual Aid". The next day Timkovskij and Beklemišev were brought in from Revel' for interrogation. Later that week Nabokov found pieces of clay outside Petraševskij's cell on which messages had been written to other prisoners. For a time the commandant thought a conspiracy might exist within the walls of Peter and Paul Fortress!

Early in the investigation, Petraševskij refused to answer questions on the grounds that to do so would be to violate his own legal rights. However, when he realized the seriousness of the charges against him, he decided to cooperate – but in his own way. In an attempt to prove the accusations ridiculous, he showered the Commission with notes and writings. He tried several distracting subterfuges: he criticized the panel's handling of the interrogation; he demanded Liprandi's removal as his interrogator, then tried to intimidate the general by threatening him with a lawsuit; he wrote Nicholas, urging him not to persecute people for their ideas; he urged the Commission to set up a Scientific Committee to spread the teachings of Fourier. He also created a spectacle by shouting to the Commissioner's demands for the introduction of a public jury system into the country. Later, he even objected to Gagarin's presence on the Commission, claiming the State Council member was an agent of the police.

In his appearances before the Commission, Petraševskij's principal defense was his aggressive attacks on the government for investigating him at all. He denied his guilt and demanded that the Commission compensate him for false arrest. It appears that by these antics Petraševskij hoped to convince the investigators that they were dealing with a fine intellect; they were not convinced. Instead, Gagarin and his colleagues were outraged that Petraševskij denied responsibility and guilt for holding radical views, and that he refused to be intimidated. The Tsar himself spent many hours reading Petraševskij's testimony, becoming increasingly incensed at the insolence of his words.

[10]   Desnitskij, "Predislovie", Delo Petraševcev, I, xviii.

Spešnev's interrogation continued through the end of May. His own culpability and that of others was revealed in his correspondence with people all over Russia. Černosvitov's visits with the *Petraševcy* the preceding winter and his plan for a secret society were discovered in Spešnev's papers. Černosvitov's arrest was consequently ordered on June 2, although the police did not find him in Siberia until July 22.

Spešnev told of the meetings at which he, Petraševskij and Černosvitov planned to organize a conspiratorial society. He interpreted for the Commissioners Mombelli's *bratstvo* and said that there was a printing press hidden in his own basement; Dubel't searched the basement, however, and reported finding no press. Spešnev's further revelations led to the formal interrogations of Mombelli, L'vov, and Konstantin Debu.

The investigation of the *Petraševcy* affair was not played out as a gentlemen's game. Many of the prisoners suffered terribly from the ordeal, which lasted from April to December of 1849. Placed in solitary confinement in the Peter and Paul Fortress, Petraševskij complained bitterly of his physical and mental agonies. Eleven years later, in Siberia, Petraševskij and L'vov described in only slightly exaggerated terms Petraševskij's suffering:

The pupils of his eyes became distended, flies and sparks appeared before his eyes. He became constipated. This caused him to have a ruptured intestine and a bursting of the perineum. There was a dreadful irritation of his hearing and sense of touch and the tiniest sound seemed like a cannon shot. He incurred a loss of will, and there was an extraordinary development of fantasies. Hallucinations, madness, and continual fainting spells ensued.[11]

In one seizure of madness, Petraševskij kicked out his cell door. For that he was put in a strait-jacket and bound to his bed for several days.

Despite his suffering, Petraševskij continued to maintain before the Commission that the government had a right to condemn him but not to render him guilty.[12] He showed great concern for his friends, requesting permission to act as their counsel for defense. Although he stated a sense of personal responsibility for their fate, Petraševskij possibly was acting to disprove his friends' suspicions that he was coldly uninterested in them.

[11] F. N. L'vov and M. V. Butaševič-Petraševskij, "Zapiska o dele Petraševcev", *Literaturnoe nasledstvo*, LXIII, p. 184.
[12] V. E. Evgrafov (ed.), *Filosofskie i obščestvenno-političeskie proizvedenija Petraševcev* (Moscow, 1953), p. 422.

In only one weak moment did Petraševskij break down before the investigators. On July 5, he requested a hearing, at which he admitted that he was a revolutionary who believed that only through revolution could Russia be saved. However, when the Commissioners asked that he put his statement in writing, Petraševskij flew into a tantrum, danced about the room, and shouted at the top of his lungs.[13] He soon quieted and sat down and composed a statement of his beliefs about revolution which was completely at odds with his oral pronouncements. It was apparent to those present that he was suffering the effects of his incarceration.

Most of the other prisoners comported themselves as Petraševskij did during the pre-trial investigation. Some tried to lighten their own guilt. Spešnev took a bizarre approach in attempting to defend those who had been implicated by his correspondence. He pleaded that the other *Petraševcy* were too untalented to form a secret society. He hoped that by persuading the Commission that only he was capable of leadership in the affair he might lift the burden from his colleagues. However, the panel only used Spešnev's testimony to ensnare still others of the *Petraševcy*.

By the end of June, the Gagarin Commission had completed the major part of its work; no new devastating evidence was to appear. Most of the case had been based on the reports of the agent Antonelli and his superior, General Liprandi. Evidence had also been supplied by other spies, including N. F. Naumov, who had opened a tobacco shop in Petraševskij's house, and Vasilij Makarovič Šapošnikov, who had also rented quarters from Petraševskij. Finally, the Commission finished its job on September 17 by turning over to the court reports on ninety-four guilty people. Added to that list were twenty-eight others whom the Commission had not investigated. The court had to pass sentence on 122 men.[14]

The Commission had been unable to prove the existence of a secret conspiratorial network across Russia. However, it had documented the *Petraševcy* attempts to form such an organization,[15] and these "tendencies" it reported to the court. General Liprandi, among others, took exception to the Commission's findings on the matter; he was convinced of the existence of a vast secret society.[16] The *Petraševcy*, he pointed

---

13   Desnitskij, *op. cit.*, I, p. 173.
14   "Predislovie", *Delo Petraševcev*, I, xx.
15   Ščegolev, *op. cit.*, III, p. 285.
16   See "Zapiski Liprandi", *Russkaja starina*, 6 (July 1872), pp. 70-85.

out, represented several social strata, making them a much more dangerous league than the Decembrists, who were of exclusively gentry background. Of course, Liprandi was smarting from having been snubbed
by the Tsar's endorsement of the Third Section in the affair. Liprandi
and his colleagues got no credit for the work done by the Ministry of
the Interior. Furthermore, he was unable to offer any hard evidence to
substantiate his disgruntlement.

Along with sending its reports to the court, the Commission also
forwarded in a list of strong recommendations to Nicholas, emphasizing
conditions in Russia which allowed a *kružok* such as the *Petraševcy* to
organize. In the future the Commission stated, extreme care should be
taken in the selection of school teachers, since so many of the *Petraševcy* were of student age. Foreign literature should be controlled by
much stronger censorship to avoid future corruption of young Russian
minds. Journalists generally were responsible for leading youth astray.
The Commission demanded that the Tsar not let Russia become corrupt
as the West was.[17]

Despite the Gagarin Commission's findings that the *Petraševcy* were
guilty of nothing more sinister than a "plot of ideas" (*zagovor idei*),
Nicholas was convinced that the young reformers posed a dangerous
threat to internal security. His prejudice against them was so strong that
he refused to let a superior criminal court try the case as he had done
in the affair of the Decembrists in 1826. Instead, he appointed a mixed
court constituted of three generals-adjutants, three senators and the
brother of the Minister of the Interior, Vasilij Perovskij, who acted as
chairman.

Of the 122 persons whose names were turned over to the court, the
government brought formal charges against only twenty-three. Ninety-
nine others were released but not pardoned. Some of them – like Saltykov, who had been in jail since 1848 for the anti-government sentiments
of his books *Contradictions* and *A Confused Affair* – were already under
the regime's thumb; those who were released entirely were put under
police surveillance for periods of a year or more, a surveillance which
amounted to nothing less than house arrest.

Nicholas' court had a relatively simple assignment. Since the pre-
trial investigation had ruled out the possibility that the accused might
be innocent, the secret trial was held only to determine the degree of
guilt of each man and fix his sentence.[18] In short order, the court handed

---

[17] Ščegolev, *op. cit.*, III, p. 288.
[18] Desnitskij, "Predislovie", I, xxi.

down fourteen death sentences and nine sentences of deportation for varying terms. But Nicholas refused to accept such leniency. He ordered a re-trial. The result of the second trial was twenty-one death sentences and two deportation decrees.

On December 19, 1849, the Tsar approved orders for the executions of twenty-one *Petraševcy*. For some, death would almost be a relief. Young Kaškin, who had earned the Tsar's enmity by being the nephew of a Decembrist plotter, had spent the entire eight months in strict solitary confinement. Vasilij Katenev's ordeal had driven him insane; although he was not sentenced, he died in a lunatic asylum in 1850. Of the twenty-three formally charged, only Černosvitov had any hope of life, and even that would be under the hardship of deportation.

When the twenty-one *Petraševcy* were led from their cells at 5.00 a.m. on December 22, they had no idea where they were being taken. They were overcome at seeing one another; some of their fellows were almost unrecognizable as a result of their suffering. More than two feet of snow covered Semenovskij Square, to which they were transported. In one corner of the square stood a wooden scaffold draped in black. Steps led up to it and a railing surrounded it. A short distance from the scaffold stood three wooden posts. Some 3,000 people filled three sides of the square, and standing guard were military units in which Mombelli, L'vov and Grigor'ev had once served.

The *Petraševcy* were led onto the scaffold and ordered into two rows of twelve and nine men facing each other. The auditor mounted the scaffold and to each of the hatless *Petraševcy* read a statement of his guilt which ended with the words "The Military-Civil Court has sentenced all to execution by shooting, and on the nineteenth of December the Tsar wrote in his own hand: 'So be it.' "[19] For the first time the prisoners learned the conclusion of their case and understood the significance of the three wooden posts.

The reading lasted about thirty minutes. Then a priest joined the men on the scaffold and called them to confession. None answered although, according to Axšarumov, Timkovskij stepped forward to kiss the priest and then returned to his place in the ranks. Petraševskij kissed the cross which the priest carried. Dostoevskij whispered to Spešnev, "We will be together with Christ."[20] Spešnev replied, "A handful of dust, I think." Grigor'ev and Mombelli crossed themselves.

The executioner passed down the lines, breaking the sword of each

[19]   Ščegolev, *op. cit.*, I, p. 206.
[20]   L'vov and Petraševskij, *op. cit.*, p. 188.

man over the man's head. The *Petraševcy* were given white shirts with caps and ordered to put them on. Then the first three of them – Petraševskij, Mombelli, and Grigor'ev[21] – were led down the steps and across to the posts to be tied facing the fifteen rifles of the firing squad. The soldiers readied their weapons and took aim at the three young men standing in the snow. But the command "Fire!" never came.

Following the first trial of the twenty-three *Petraševcy*, a member of the Military-Civil Court had remarked that the whole affair was not as important as the regime had first imagined. The Tsar had ordered the punishments increased, the judge intimated, because he wished to manifest his mercy: "the sovereign likes to pardon".[22]

There was also another element of the Tsar's early decision not to have the *Petraševcy* shot. In July Russian troops had helped the Austrian army put down a revolt in Hungary. Those Hungarian officers who had surrendered to the Russian general were executed upon their release to the Austrians, contrary to a promise made to the Russians by the Austrians. At the same time, Hungarian civilians who had surrendered directly to the Austrians received much lighter punishment. The Tsar, declaring such actions "unheard of", was insulted.[23] He wished to shame the Austrians by his display of magnaminity toward the *Petraševcy* conspirators. The 'execution' had been a carefully staged farce.

The three *Petraševcy* were led back to the scaffold, where the reprieve was announced to the group. In the name of the Emperor, the death sentences were commuted to varying periods of exile in Siberia. Petraševskij received a life sentence in the mines. Mombelli and Grigor'ev were each given fifteen years in the mines; L'vov got twelve years, Spešnev got ten. Jastžembskij received six years of labor in a factory, Dostoevskij and Durov got four years each in factory labor and Tol' got two years. Timkovskij got six years on a convict labor gang, while Axšarumov, Konstantin Debu, and Filippov got four years. Ippolit Debu got two years at convict labor. Golovinskij, Evropeus, Kaškin, Pleščeev, Xanykov, and Šapošnikov were made privates in a line battalion. Pal'm was pardoned but transferred from the Guards into the army. Černosvitov was sent to Keksgol'mskaja Fortress to re-

[21]   Ščegolev, *op. cit.*, I, p. 202.
[22]   V. I. Semevskij, "Sledstvie po delu Petraševcev", *Russkie zapiski*, 11 (November 1916), p. 31.
[23]   Ščegolev, *op. cit.*, I, p. 97.

main under surveillance. The list of sentences was published the next day in the *Russian Veteran* (*Russkij invalid*).[24]

The prisoners were then forced to put back on their prison garb. A heavy snow was falling as two blacksmiths appeared to fit iron fetters on Petraševskij's legs. In a gesture perhaps symbolic of the futility of the whole affair, Petraševskij took a smith's hammer and drove the nails into the fetters himself. A hooded sleigh drove up to the scaffold. As Petraševskij shuffled down the line of men to the sleigh, each in turn said goodbye to him, many with tears in their eyes. As Axšarumov said of the moment, "This was the first time I ever really loved him."[25] And so Mixail Petraševskij, at age twenty-eight, was on his way to a Siberian exile from which he would never return. His many pleas for clemency would not be answered, not even by Alexander II's general amnesty of 1856. In fact, he would be repeatedly moved farther and farther into the Siberian wilderness, until his death at Bel'skij in the Enisej region in 1866.

Within a few minutes after Petraševskij's departure, the other *Petraševcy* were escorted away in groups of two and three to begin their imprisonments. The convoy of sleighs moving toward Siberia formed a long, dark line across the Russian snow.

The great tragedy of these men was their youth. They were intelligent, educated, idealistic, and, to a great degree, innocent of the monstrous proportions of the task they had plotted for themselves. Their failure was inevitable. And they paid for their *naiveté* with their most productive years. Most of them were under thirty in 1849; Kaškin was barely twenty. Few returned to prominence, or even to useful lives. Some later used the experience of Siberian exile to good advantage in their writings and in literature found a vent for their social consciences. But others were forever stunted. What heights might a promising poet such as Durov have reached if he had been free during his productive twenties? Of the *Petraševcy* who escaped sentencing to Siberia, only one gained political power and prominence. A. P. Beklemišev became a provincial governor under Alexander II. The returned exiles found the doors of officialdom closed to them.

And to what final purpose did the regime's prosecution of the *Petraševcy* succeed? One of the Third Section agents who was on the square the day of the 'execution' reported that the regime had failed to teach the *Petraševcy* any sort of lesson. "I must say", the agent said, "that

[24] Lejkina-Svirskaja, *op. cit.*, p. 145.
[25] Ščegolev, *op. cit.*, I, p. 209.

there was not noticeable among the criminals that reverential emotion and fear that one ought to expect in such a sorrowful moment of human life." Petraševskij, he said, was the most insolent of all. The young man whose idealism and naive social fervor had led him and twenty-one of his friends to the brink of death stood on the scaffold and snickered, "Lord, how ridiculous we must be in these costumes." [26]

[26]   *Političeskie processy Nikolaevskoj èpoxi: Petraševcy* (Moscow, 1907), pp. 153-154.

BIBLIOGRAPHY

PRIMARY SOURCES

Bel'čikov, Nikolaj Fedorovič, *Dostoevskij v processe Petraševcev* (Moscow: Izda-tel'stvo Akademii Nauk, 1936).

Considérant, Victor, *Destinée sociale*, 2 volumes (Paris: Bureau de la Phalange, 1837).

Desnitskij, Vasilij Alekseevič (ed.), *Delo Petraševcev*, 3 volumes (Moscow: Izda-tel'stvo Akademii Nauk, 1937, 1941, 1951).

Evgrafov, Vasilij Evgrafovič (ed.), *Filosofskie i obščestvenno-političeskie proizve-denija Petraševcev* (Moscow: Gospolitizdat, 1953).

Feuerbach, Ludwig Andreas, *The Essence of Christianity*, trans. Marian Evans from the seventh German edition (New York: Calvin Blanchard, 1855).

Fourier, Charles, *Œuvres complètes de Charles Fourier*, 6 volumes in 8, second edition (Paris: Bureau de la Phalange, 1841-1845).

Geršenzon, Mixail Osipovič (ed.), *Russkaja byl': Èpoxa Nikolaja I*, 7 volumes (Moscow: Obrazovanie, VII, 1910).

Grigor'ev, Apollon, "Dva ègoizma", *Izbrannye proizvedenija*, ed. Boris Kosteljanec (Leningrad: Sovetskij Pisatel', 1959), pp. 185-268.

Jaxontov, Aleksandr Nikolaevič, "Vospominanija carskosel'skogo liceista", *Rus-skaja starina*, 10 (October 1888), pp. 101-124.

Karmannyj slovar' inostrannyx slov, vošedšix v sostav russkogo jazyka, 2 volumes (St. Petersburg: Nikolaj Sergeevič Kirilov, 1845-1846).

Kuz'min, Pavel Alekseevič, "Iz zapisok Kuz'mina", *Russkaja starina*, 2, 4 (February, April 1895), pp. 71-86, 154-173.

Liprandi, Ivan Petrovič, "Zapiski Liprandi", *Russkaja starina*, 6 (July 1872), pp. 70-85.

L'vov, Fedor Nikolaevič, and Mixail Vasil'evič Butaševič-Petraševskij, "Zapiska o dele Petraševcev", *Literaturnoe nasledstvo*, LXIII (Moscow: Izdatel'stvo Akademii Nauk, 1956), pp. 165-190.

Miljutin, Vladimir Alekseevič, *Izbrannye proizvedenija*, ed. Izrael Grigor'evič Bljumen (Moscow: Gosizdat, 1946).

Pal'm, Aleksandr Ivanovič, *Aleksej Slobodin* (St. Petersburg: n.p., 1873).

Poèty-Petraševcy, ed. Vasilij Leonidovič Komarovič (Leningrad: Sovetskij Pisatel', 1957).

Političeskie processy Nikolaevskoj èpoxi: Petraševcy (Moscow: V. Sablin, 1907).

Porošin, Sof'ja Stepanovna, "Professor Viktor Porošin", *Russkaja starina*, 4 (April 1892), pp. 121-140.

Raeff, Marc (ed.), *Russian Intellectual History: An Anthology* (New York: Har-court, Brace and World, Inc., 1966).

Rubinštejn, Anton Grigor'evič, "Vospominanija A. G. Rubinštejna", *Russkaja starina*, 11 (November 1889), pp. 517-578.

Saint-Simon, Claude Henri de, *Nouveau Christianisme* (Paris: Au bureau du globe, 1832).

Saltykov, Mixail Evgrafovič, *Za rubežom* (Moscow: Gosizdat, 1950).

Ščegolev, Pavel Eliseevič (ed.), *Petraševcy*, 3 volumes (Moscow: Gospolitizdat, 1926-1928).

Semevskaja, Aleksandra Vasil'evna, "Zametka o M. V. Butaševič-Petraševskom", *Russkaja starina*, 12 (December 1901), pp. 493-494.

Sismondi, Jean Charles Leonard Somonde de, *Nouveaux principes d'économie politique; ou de la richesse dans ses rapports avec la population*, 2 volumes, third edition (Geneva: Edition Jeheber, 1951-1953).

Veselovskij, Konstantin Stepanovič, "Vospominanija o nekotoryx licejskix tovariščax", *Russkaja starina*, 5 (May 1900), pp. 449-456.

Vidal, Francis, *De la répartition des richesses* (Paris: Capelle, 1846).

Zotov, Vladimir Rafailovič, "Peterburg v sorokovyx godax", *Istoričeskij vestnik*, 6 (June 1890), pp. 536-554.

SECONDARY SOURCES

Annenkov, Pavel Vasil'evič, *Vospominanija i kritičeskie očerki* (St. Petersburg: Tipografija M. M. Stašulevič, 1881).

Balabanov, Mixail Solomonovič, *Istorija revoljucionnogo dviženija v Rossii ot Dekabristov k 1905 godu* (Kharkov: Gosizdat Ukrainy, 1925).

Barruel, Augustin de, *Mémoirs pour servir à l'historie du Jacobinisme* (London: P. Le Boussonnier & Co., 1797-1798).

Berlin, Isaiah, "Russia and 1848", *Slavonic and East European Review*, XXVI (April 1948), pp. 341-360.

Bezrodnyj, A. V., "K biografii Petraševskogo", *Istoričeskij vestnik*, 1 (January 1901), pp. 225-229.

Bourgin, Hubert, *Fourier: Contribution à l'étude du socialisme Français* (Paris: Société Novelle de libraire et d'édition, 1905).

——, *Victor Considérant: son œuvre* (Lyon: Imprimeries réunies, 1909).

Brower, Daniel, "The Tragedy of a Russian Reformer: The Political Ideals and Actions of Mikhail Petrashevskii" (unpublished master's thesis, Columbia University, 1959).

Brown, Edward J., *Stankevich and His Moscow Circle, 1830-1840* (Stanford: Stanford University Press, 1966).

Burcev, Vladimir L'vovič, *Za sto let, 1800-1896* (London: Free Press Fund, 1897).

Cantagrel, François Jean Felix, *Le fou du Palais-Royale* (Paris: Librairie phalanstérienne, 1841).

"Cenzura v carstvovanie imperatora Nikolaja pervogo", *Russkaja starina*, 8 (August 1903), pp. 405-437.

Demor, Vladimir Petrovič, *M. V. Petraševskij: Biografičeskij očerk* (St. Petersburg: Gosizdat, 1920).

Èpoxa feodalizma, čast' vtoraja, 1800-1861, ed. A. I. Paškov, = Volume I of *Istorija russkoj èkonomičeskoj mysli*, 4 volumes (Moscow: Izdatel'stvo social'no-èkonomičeskoj literatury, 1958).

Fadner, Frank, *Seventy Years of Pan-Slavism in Russia, Karamzin to Danilevskij, 1800-1870* (Washington: Georgetown University Press, 1961).

Gercen, Aleksandr Ivanovič, *Polnoe sobranie sočinenij i pisem*, ed. Mixail Konstantovič Lemke, 22 volumes (Petrograd: Gosizdat, 1919-1925).

——, "Petrashevsky", *Revue politique et littéraire (Revue bleue)*, XLVI (November-December 1908), pp. 387-389; 417-422.

Gernet, Mixail Nikolaevič, *Istorija carskoj tjurmy*, 5 volumes (Moscow: Gosizdat, 1961).

Grossman, Leonid Petrovič, *Dostoevskij* (Moscow: "Molodaja Gvardija", 1963).

Haxthausen, August, *Studien über die inneren Zustände des Volkslebens und insbesondere die ländlichen Einrichtungen Russlands*, 3 volumes (Hanover: Hahn, 1847).

Kaplan, Frederick I., "Russian Fourierism of the 1840's: A Contrast to Hertsen's Westernism", *American Slavic and East European Review*, XVII (1958), pp. 161-172.

Kuklin, Georgij Arkad'evič, *Petraševcy* (Geneva: G. A. Kuklin, 1906).

Lejkina, Vera Romanovna, *Petraševcy* (Moscow: Gosudarstvennaja Tipografija, 1924).

Lejkina-Svirskaja, Vera Romanovna, "Revoljucionnaja praktika Petraševcev", *Istoričeskie zapiski*, XLVII (1954), pp. 181-223.

——, *Petraševcy* (Moscow: Prosveščenie, 1965).

——, "Formirovanie raznočinskoj intelligencii v Rossii v 40-x godax XIX veka", *Istorija SSSR*, I (1958), pp. 83-104.

——, "O xaraktere kružkov Petraševcev", *Voprosy istorii*, 4 (April 1956), pp. 96-106.

——, "Pervyj ètap osvoboditel'nogo dviženija v Rossii v istoričeskoj literature, izdannoj v 1956-1959", *Istorija SSSR*, 1 (January 1961), pp. 167-176.

Lemke, Mixail Konstantovič, *Nikolaevskie žandarmy i literatura, 1826-1855* (St. Petersburg: Izdanie Vtoroe, 1909).

Leroux, Pierre, and Jean Reynaud, *Encyclopédie nouvelle; ou dictionnaire philosophique, scientifique, littéraire et industriel, offrant le tableau des connaissances humaines au dix-neuvième siècle, par une société des savants et de littérateurs*, 2 volumes (Paris: C. Gosselin, 1836).

Makašin, Sergej Aleksandrovič, *Saltykov-Ščedrin*, 2 volumes (Moscow: Goslitizdat, 1951).

Malia, Martin, "What is the Intelligentsia?", *The Russian Intelligentsia*, ed. Richard Pipes (New York: Columbia University Press, 1961).

——, *Alexander Herzen and the Birth of Russian Socialism* (Cambridge: Harvard University Press, 1961).

"Malthus", *Encyclopedia Britannica*, 13th edition, 28 volumes, XVII (1926), p. 515.

Manuel, Frank, *The Prophets of Paris* (New York: Harper & Row, 1962).

Mart'janov, Pavel K., "V perelome veka", *Istoričeskij vestnik*, 10 and 11 (October and November 1895), pp. 126-148; 434-463.

Močul'skij, Konstantin Vasil'evič, *Dostoevskij, žizn' i tvorčestvo* (Paris: YMCA Press, 1947).

Monas, Sydney, *The Third Section: Police and Society in Russia under Nicholas I* (Cambridge: Harvard University Press, 1961).

Oksman, Julian Grigor'evič, "Mery Nikolaevskoj cenzury protiv Fur'erizma", *Golos minuvšago*, 5 and 6 (May and June 1917), pp. 69-72.

Pažitnov, Konstantin Alekseevič, *Razvitie socialističeskix idej v Rossii* (Petrograd: Izdatel'stvo "Byloe", 1924).

Pearson, Charles, *The Politico-Social Ideas of Lamennais* (New York: New York University Press, 1936).

"Petraševskij – Petraševcy", *Bol'šaja sovetskaja ènciklopedija*, second edition, 51 volumes, XXXII (1954), pp. 589-592.

Polievktov, Mixail, *Nikolaj I* (Moscow: Izdatel'stvo Sabašnakovyx, 1918).

Popper, Karl R., *The Open Society and Its Enemies*, 2 volumes (New York: Harper & Row, 1963).

Proudhon, Joseph Pierre, *Qu'est-ce que la propriété?*, second edition (Paris: Garnier frères, 1848).

Pushkarev, Sergei, *The Emergence of Modern Russia, 1801-1917*, trans. Robert H. McNeal and Tova Yedlin (New York: Rinehart & Winston, 1963).

Pypin, Aleksandr Nikolaevič, *Moi zametki* (Moscow: Izdanie L. E. Bucheima, 1910).

Rajskij, Leonid, *Social'noe vozzrenie Petraševcev: Očerk iz istorii utopičeskogo socializma v Rossii* (Leningrad: Priboj, 1927).

Riasanovsky, Nicholas V., "Fourierism in Russia: An Estimate of the Petrashevcy", *American Slavic and East European Review* (October 1953), pp. 289-302.

Semevskij, Vasilij Ivanovič, "Petraševcy i krest'janskij vopros", *Velikaja reforma* (Moscow: Tipografija I. D. Sytina, 1911).

——, "Sledstvie po delu Petraševcev", *Russkie zapiski*, 11 (November 1916), pp. 18-51.

——, *Krepostnoe pravo i krest'janskaja reforma v proizvedenijax Mixaila Evgrafoviča Saltykova* (St. Petersburg: Donskaja Reč', 1906).

——, "Petraševcy A. P. Beklemišev i K. I. Timkovskij", *Vestnik Evropy*, 10 (November 1916), pp. 57-103.

——, "M. V. Butaševič-Petraševskij", *Bol'šaja ènciklopedija*, ed. A. N. Južakov, 20 volumes, IV (St. Petersburg, 1896), pp. 132-135.

——, *Krest'janskij vopros v XVIII i v pervoj polovine XIX veka*, 2 volumes (St. Petersburg: Obščestvennaja Pol'za, 1888).

——, *Sobranie sočinenij: M. V. Butaševič-Petraševskij i Petraševcy*, ed. Vasilij Vasil'evič Vodovozov, II (Moscow: Zadruga, 1922).

——, *Iz istorii obščestvennyx idej v Rossii v konce 1840-x godov* (Rostov na Donu: Izdatel'stvo Paramonova Donskaja Reč', 1905).

——, "Kružok Kaškina", *Golos minuvšago*, 4 (April 1916), pp. 174-192.

——, "D. D. Axšarumov i A. I. Evropeus", *Golos minuvšago*, 3 (March 1916), pp. 46-48.

——, "Propaganda Petraševcev v učebnyx zavedenijax", *Golos minuvšago*, 2 (February 1917), pp. 138-169.

——, "A. V. Xanykov", *Golos minuvšago*, 2 (February 1916), pp. 45-56.

——, "N. S. Kaškin", *Golos minuvšago*, 2 (February 1916), pp. 41-45.

——, "K. M. i I. M. Debu", *Golos minuvšago*, 2 (February 1916), pp. 56-61.

——, "Durov", *Ènciklopedičeskij slovar'*, seventh edition, 48 volumes, XIX (Moscow: "Br. A i I. Granat i Ko.", 1914), p. 167.

——, "Grigor'ev", *Ènciklopedičeskij slovar'*, seventh edition, 48 volumes, XVIII (Moscow: "Br. A i I. Granat i Ko.", 1914), p. 127.

——, "Petraševskij – Petraševcy", *Ènciklopedičeskij slovar'*, seventh edition, 48 volumes, XXXII (Moscow: "Br. A i I. Granat i Ko.", 1914), pp. 79-86.

——, "Golovinskij", *Ènciklopedičeskij slovar'*, seventh edition, 48 volumes, XV (Moscow: "Br. A i I. Granat i Ko.", 1914), p. 333.

——, "Tol'", *Ènciklopedičeskij slovar'*, 41 volumes, XXXIII (St. Petersburg: F. A. Brockhaus and I. A. Efron, 1901), p. 438.

——, "Vlijanie Fur'erizma v Rossii", *Ènciklopedičeskij slovar'*, 41 volumes, XXXVI (St. Petersburg: F. A. Brockhaus and I. A. Efron, 1902), pp. 903-912.

——, "Spešnev", *Ènciklopedičeskij slovar'*, 41 volumes, XXXI (St. Petersburg: F. A. Brockhaus and I. A. Efron, 1900), p. 316.

——, "Petraševcy", *Ènciklopedičeskij slovar'*, 41 volumes, XXIII (St. Petersburg: F. A. Brockhaus and I. A. Efron, 1898), pp. 450-451.

Šilov, Aleksej Alekseevič, *Čto čitat' po istorii Russkogo revoljucionnogo dviženija* (St. Petersburg: Gosizdat, 1922).

Sokolovskij, Mixail Mixailovič, "Delo Petraševcev kak èpizod v istorii obščestvennogo dviženija v Rossii", *Russkaja starina*, 11 (November 1905), pp. 351-365.

Sourine, George, *Le Fourierisme en Russie* (Paris: Paul Dupont, 1936).

Strauss, David Friedrich, *The Life of Jesus*, trans. Marian Evans, 2 volumes (New York: Calvin Blanchard, 1856).

Tocqueville, Alexis de, *L'ancien régime* (Paris: Librairie Gallimard, 1952).

Tol', Feliks Gustafovič, *Nastol'nyj slovar' dlja spravok po vsem otrasljam znanii (Spravočnyj ènciklopedičeskij leksikon)*, 3 volumes (St. Petersburg: Feliks Gustafovič Tol', 1863-1866).

Valevskij, M. S., "Volnenija krest'jan v zaural'skoj časti Permskogo kraja v 1842-1843", *Russkaja starina*, 11 and 12 (November and December 1879), pp. 411-432; 627-646.

Venturi, Franco, *Roots of Revolution*, trans. Francis Haskell (New York: Alfred Knopf, 1960).

Volgin, Vjačeslav Petrovič, "Social'noe učenie Vejtlinga", *Voprosy istorii*, 8 (August 1961), pp. 7-26.

Weitling, Wilhelm Christian, *Die Menscheit wie sie ist und wie sie sein sollte*, fourth edition (New York: Die Bibliothek der Arbeiten, 1854).

——, *Čelovečestvo kakovo ono est' i kakovym dolžno byt'* (St. Petersburg: Biblioteka "Prosveščenie", 1906).

——, *Garantien der Harmonie und Freiheit*, second edition (Hamburg: Verlage des Verfassers, 1849).

Wittke, Carl, *The Utopian Communist: A Biography of Wilhelm Christian Weitling, Nineteenth Century Reformer* (Baton Rouge: Louisiana State University Press, 1950).

Yarmolinsky, Avrahm, *Road to Revolution* (London: Cassell and Co., 1957).

Zil'berfarb, Iogann Isaakovič, *Social'naja filosofija Šarlja Fur'e i ee mesto v istorii socialističeskoj mysli pervoj poloviny XIX veka* (Moscow: Izdatel'stvo Nauka, 1964).

——, "Idei Fur'e v Rossii v 30-40-x godax XIX veka", *Istoričeskie zapiski*, XXVII (1948), pp. 240-265.

——, "Social'naja filosofija Šarlja Fur'e kak predmet istoričeskogo issledovanija", *Voprosy istorii*, 5 (May 1956), pp. 58-76.

INDEX